Embracing Self-Compassion: Meditation Journeys for Self-Kindness

Anne E. Beall, PhD

EMBRACING SELF-COMPASSION: MEDITATION
JOURNEYS FOR SELF-KINDNESS

Cover Designed by Atiq Ahmed.

All images, including cover image, generated with
123rf.com

ISBN: 979-8-990192904 (Paperback)
ISBN: 979-8-990192911 (Hard Cover)

To Xander and Max, whose sensitivity, intelligence, and kindness inspire me every day.

Creating a wonderful family with you both has been one of my greatest blessings.

Contents

Acknowledgments

This book would not have been possible without the support and contributions of many individuals. First, I would like to thank Judi Goshen, whose encouragement and feedback guided me throughout this journey. Her careful reading and insights led to significant revisions, enhancing the book's quality.

My gratitude also goes to Jackie Short, my first client and a friend of thirty years. Her valuable feedback and encouragement helped me tremendously. I am deeply thankful to Christine Avallone for helping me think through some meditations that weren't quite working. Avesha Michael also provided invaluable feedback, helping me see the bigger picture. Marcia Harris offered a fresh perspective that led to a new meditation journey. I also appreciate Jeff Baltes for his thoughtful input, and Leo Bacino, whose meticulous reading influenced several key changes. His insights were valuable in refining the length of the meditations and adding further explication where it was needed.

I'd also like to thank my husband, Michael, who is my rock—my anchor, my personal chef, and my biggest cheerleader. He has encouraged me in all my pursuits. He calls me 'DynaGirl' because he believes I'm full of energy and can do anything. Sometimes, I almost believe him.

Finally, I extend my heartfelt thanks to everyone who shared how this book could benefit them or their loved ones. And to all the readers who have purchased my books, you are the reason I write every day.

—Anne E. Beall

Introduction: Overview of Self-Compassion

My father always called me his "no mercy kid." It was a compliment, but it also communicated his high expectations and his reluctance to go easy on me. Whenever heavy furniture needed to be moved, he turned to me. This idea became a core part of my early self-concept—I demanded much from myself and was unkind when I failed to meet my expectations. I berated myself when I fell short with grades or if I had made a thoughtless or embarrassing comment.

Not only did I set high standards for myself, I also expected much from others, letting no one off the hook. This left me perpetually disappointed and unhappy. Life was not what I wanted, and the reason seemed clear: no one, including me, met my expectations. This attitude made life difficult for me and for those who loved me. Among the last things my father said before his passing was, "Go easy on other people. Don't be so harsh."

As I've aged, I regret my past mistakes and realize that life is much better when I'm compassionate towards myself and others. But these patterns are deeply ingrained, and cultivating self-compassion is not a simple task. I've learned that it involves multiple steps and letting go of long-held beliefs from my childhood. It requires time and practice, but it's worth the effort. I'm certainly much happier with myself, with others, and with life now that I'm trying to be more compassionate. And I'm ready to guide you on this journey, focusing on areas where people are often the hardest on themselves. Before I start, I'd like to discuss what self-compassion actually means.

Self-compassion involves treating yourself with the same kindness, concern, and support you'd offer a good friend. When facing difficult moments, instead of harshly judging yourself, self-compassion allows you to be understanding and nurturing. It's about recognizing that imperfection, failure, and life's challenges are inevitable parts of our human experience.

According to Kristin Neff (2011), an expert in this field, self-compassion requires three key components: self-kindness, common humanity, and mindfulness.

Self-kindness vs. Self-judgment: Self-kindness is the practice of treating yourself with the same compassion that you would offer someone you love. It involves extending warmth and understanding to yourself, especially during challenging moments. Instead of harsh self-criticism and judgment, it encourages a gentle and forgiving attitude. It's about recognizing that being human means making mistakes, facing imperfections, and sometimes falling short of our own expectations. Self-kindness invites us to embrace these moments with tenderness and self-acceptance, understanding that it's completely okay not to be perfect.

Common humanity vs. Isolation: This concept acknowledges our shared human experience of suffering, challenges, and mistakes. It reminds us we are not alone in our struggles; rather, we are connected because we all face difficulties. In times of hardship, it's common to feel isolated and believe that we are the only ones going through a particular ordeal. However, others have experienced similar pain and challenges. This knowledge fosters a sense of belonging and empathy, reducing the sense of isolation, which encourages us to reach out for support and connection when needed.

Mindfulness vs. Over-identification: Mindfulness is the practice of cultivating a present-moment awareness of our thoughts, emotions, and sensations that allows us to observe them without over-identifying with them. We can see our negative emotions without becoming overwhelmed or entangled in them. Instead of reacting impulsively to our inner experiences, mindfulness encourages us to view things without judgement. It's about creating space between our thoughts and reactions, which empowers us to respond with clarity and wisdom. By practicing mindfulness, we can navigate challenging emotions with greater ease, fostering emotional resilience and self-awareness.

Extensive research has shown the impact of self-compassion on people's lives. It has been consistently linked to improved mental health through a reduction in anxiety, depression, and stress (Bates et al., 2021; Bui et al., 2021; Neff, Kirkpatrick & Rude). And because it reduces the burden of self-blame, it becomes a vital component of healing from trauma (Germer & Neff, 2015). Furthermore, self-compassion enhances emotional resilience, allowing individuals to navigate life's hurdles with grace and to find support in moments of difficulty. Self-compassion also influences physical health, fostering lower inflammation, improved immune function, and healthier lifestyles.

Moreover, those who cultivate self-compassion are happier, have higher life satisfaction, and greater overall well-being (Mülazım & Eldeleklioğlu, 2016; Neff, Rude, & Kirkpatrick, 2007). They have a brighter outlook, are free from harsh self-criticism, and are better equipped for the difficulties of life. Importantly, self-compassion nurtures healthier relationships, promoting empathy, forgiveness, and understanding towards oneself and others (Neff & Beretvas, 2013). It's likely the foundation for strong and happy relationships.

And if that weren't enough, self-compassion is linked to achievement because it fuels motivation to persevere through challenges (Neff et al., 2005). Contrary to the belief that lacking compassion for oneself can spur greater success, the reality is quite the opposite. Research shows that high levels of self-criticism can erode self-confidence, leading to increased anxiety and reduced performance (Powers et al., 2007). Conversely, cultivating self-compassion fosters positive emotions that are likely to lead to enhanced productivity (Oswald et al., 2015). For those weighed down by perfectionism, self-compassion offers relief. It encourages a gentler approach to oneself and a reduced fear of failure (Neff et al., 2005). In a society that places immense pressure on the pursuit of success and perfection, self-compassion is essential because it reminds us we are human, and that all of us deserve kindness.

Self-compassion also appears to enhance physical health by fostering a kinder attitude toward illness. Researchers have found that individuals with higher self-compassion are more likely to seek medical attention sooner and engage in health-promoting behaviors compared to those with lower self-compassion (Terry et al., 2013). People who are self-compassionate tend to adopt a more proactive approach to their health, they practice benevolent self-talk and are motivated to be kind to themselves.

Thus, self-compassion affects our mental and physical health, emotional well-being, and the quality of our relationships. It is the cornerstone of a kinder, gentler, and more fulfilling life.

But how can we enhance our self-compassion? It may seem simple, but our deeply ingrained thought patterns are not always easy to see and to change. We frequently hear that inner voice telling us we fall short or never quite measure up. These critical voices could have developed from people we knew, like a parent or teacher, or they could have arisen from our own high self-expectations, as they did for me.

To change these entrenched patterns, we need to shift our thinking. One way to achieve this is through guided meditation journeys, which help us relax, alter our perspectives, and incorporate a more compassionate viewpoint into our minds.

Each chapter of this book addresses a different aspect of life where we may struggle to be compassionate towards ourselves. From our body image, to our personal relationships, to our past mistakes, to aging.

This journey involves embracing every aspect of yourself with kindness and understanding. It's about becoming your own ally, especially during difficult moments. Through the practice of self-compassion, you can discover enhanced peace, joy, and fulfillment in your life.

However, it's important to note that this approach doesn't advocate for settling for less, abandoning goals, or striving for mediocrity. Instead, it encourages embracing life to the fullest, understanding that some things are beyond our control and only focusing on what we can change. Being compassionate with oneself along this life journey enhances the overall experience.

How to Use this Book

This book will take you on a journey toward becoming more self-compassionate. Here's how you can make the most of this book.

- **Approach with Openness**: Enter this journey with an open mind and heart. Be willing to explore new perspectives and challenge long-held beliefs about yourself.
- **Consistent Practice**: Self-compassion is like a muscle—the more you practice, the stronger it becomes.
- **Meditate**: Each chapter includes meditation journeys. You can listen to them on the audiobook, or you can read them. I personally like to grasp the essence of a meditation and then sit quietly to meditate and envision what I've read.
- **Be Patient with Yourself**: Cultivating self-compassion is a journey, not a destination. It's not always easy. Be patient and gentle with yourself as you navigate this process.
- **Revisit as Needed**: You might find certain chapters more relevant at different times. Revisit sections as needed, using this book when you need a little help.

The next meditation journeys will help you increase your overall self-compassion. In subsequent chapters, you'll find ones tailored for specific areas, such as body image, relationships, and more. I recommend beginning with this general meditation.

Meditation Journey One: Starlit Reflection

Before you begin this meditation, take a moment to reflect on some criticisms you have of yourself. Hold these thoughts gently, because we will explore and address them during this journey.

Begin by finding a tranquil space where you can sit comfortably, free from distractions. Take a series of deep, soothing breaths, focusing on centering yourself in the present moment. Release the concerns of the day and grant yourself permission to fully immerse yourself.

Imagine standing under a vast, starlit sky on a calm and peaceful night. The darkness of the night is soothing and comforting. Overhead, countless stars twinkle brightly, casting their radiant light upon you. Feel the serenity of this moment enveloping your entire being.

As you stand in this tranquil space, you feel the soft, cool grass beneath your feet. Let your senses absorb the feeling of the earth supporting you, reminding you of your intrinsic connection to the natural world. Inhale deeply, breathing in the crisp, clean air, allowing it to fill your lungs with a sense of renewal.

As you relax on this calm night, focus your attention inward. Within each of us, there are critical voices that sometimes grow loud and that put us down. In this moment of serenity, gently allow yourself to acknowledge the criticisms that often echo in your mind. These might concern your abilities, decisions, or aspects of your personality or appearance.

Consider these criticisms. Focus on the one that is most frequent or most painful—the one you wish wasn't part of your life. Perhaps you feel bad about this aspect of yourself and wish you could be different. This could be something you deeply wish you could change. Take a moment to identify this criticism and visualize placing it into a bubble in front of you. See this bubble with the criticism inside it, floating there, separated from you, allowing you to examine it with detachment.

Now, look at this criticism. How long have you been carrying it around? Do you recall who first said this about you? Look at this statement and ask yourself if it is completely true. Is it possible that you have labeled yourself in this way and that it's exaggerated? Is it possible that you have been carrying something around that you haven't fully questioned?

Challenge the criticism by comparing it to real-life evidence from your experiences. Recall instances where this criticism was not accurate. Think about times when you behaved or acted in ways that contradict this belief. Imagine you are a fair and wise judge, assessing the validity of this claim. Does this criticism truly represent you, or are you being overly hard on yourself? Take the time to objectively evaluate the criticism you have placed in the bubble. Remember that no single criticism fully describes a human being—we are complex. Although there may be instances that seem to support this belief, there are probably many more that do not. This criticism may not be an accurate representation of you.

Now, see this bubble floating in the air before you. Notice how it shimmers with the reflections of the moonlight, encasing the self-critical thought you've acknowledged. Observe it for a moment, seeing it as a separate entity from your self—external and not embedded within you. Look at this bubble and recognize that what it contains does not fully describe you. It has been weighing you down and making you feel negatively about yourself. It is in this bubble now, and you are going to release it into the night air.

Take a deep, grounding breath, feeling the cool night air fill your lungs. As you exhale, imagine this bubble rising into the air. You let this criticism go as it rises further, carried by the gentle night breeze. As it ascends, you say, "That is not a true representation of me. I'm letting it go." With each breath, it floats higher and farther, its size diminishing, its form becoming less defined. As it rises, recognize that this bubble, like your critical thoughts, does not have to define you or remain attached to you. You have the power to let it go.

Watch as the bubble ascends into the vastness of the night sky, a boundless expanse that welcomes and absorbs it, making it part of something larger while it lessens its presence in your life. As the bubble rises, it lightens your mental load, reaffirming your ability to separate from negative self-judgments and move towards self-acceptance.

As you gaze up at the starlit sky, the bubble gets smaller and smaller and smaller. You watch as it rises and rises. Eventually it disappears, and when you can no longer see it, you feel better. You realize that you have been hard on yourself, and you feel lighter and freer.

You notice the constellations and the intricate patterns they form. Each star in the night sky is like a unique facet of your being—distinct, radiant, and contributing to the rich tapestry of your life. Like these stars, you possess your own brilliance, strengths, and unique qualities. Embrace and celebrate the uniqueness that you bring to the world, just as you admire the diversity and beauty of the stars above.

This starlit sanctuary is always accessible to you. It serves as a refuge—a place you can return to whenever you need to let go of harsh self-criticisms.

Now it's time to leave. Gently bring your awareness back to your current surroundings, while retaining these feelings as you go into your day or evening.

Meditation Journey Two: Forest of Compassion

Before you begin this meditation, think about a time when you didn't meet your expectations, or you did something you regretted afterward. We will explore this memory on this journey.

Begin this meditation by finding a quiet and comfortable spot where you can sit undisturbed. Allow yourself the freedom to be fully present in this moment, away from the hustle and bustle of daily life. Take a deep, calming breath. As you exhale, feel any tension or stress leaving your body. Take several more deep breaths and let yourself fully relax. There is nowhere you need to be right now but here.

Imagine you are at the edge of a tranquil forest. Trees tower above you, their leaves displaying a spectrum of green hues, from light jade to deep emerald. You hear the gentle rustling of leaves in the breeze, a soft whisper that seems to welcome you. They stand as silent guardians in this serene place. Beneath your feet, the forest floor is a lush carpet of moss. You marvel at the towering trees around you, their bark a mosaic of deep browns and grays, rough to the touch. Warm sunlight filters through the leaves, casting a dappled glow that dances across the ground, creating a serene and magical atmosphere.

As you walk along the path into the forest, notice the sensations under your feet. It feels as though you are walking on a plush, natural mat. The moss is a reminder of how the earth supports you with each step. You inhale deeply, breathing in the fresh air of the forest. Let it fill your lungs and relax you.

You look around and take in the beauty of your surroundings. The trees reach skyward, their branches swaying gracefully. Each plant, each tree, plays a vital role in this ecosystem, just as you play an important role in the world around you. Some trees are ancient— their trunks are enormous, reaching skyward with a sense of timeless strength. Others are smaller, young saplings scattered across the forest floor, each holding the promise of the future.

As you continue your walk, you come across a massive tree that has split into two enormous trunks. You touch the rough, deep brown bark and marvel at how this ancient tree, joined at the roots, has become two separate beings reaching for the sun. The texture under your fingers is a testament to the passage of time, a connection to the enduring strength and resilience of nature.

As you continue along this path through the tranquil forest, allow yourself a moment to pause and reflect. Gently bring to mind a specific instance from your past where you feel you didn't meet your own expectations. Maybe it was a time when an unintended mistake led to embarrassment, a missed opportunity, or a misunderstanding with someone close to you.

In this tranquil forest, hold this memory in your heart with tenderness. Think about the feelings that arise in response to it. Look at this memory without judgment, but with curiosity. Consider what led up to this situation and the many things that were happening at that time.

Now, visualize a beloved figure from your life appearing on your path in this forest. This person may be a family member, a dear friend, a mentor, or even a spiritual guide—someone who embodies unconditional love and deep empathy. See them approaching you on the forest path with a warm, understanding smile. Their eyes reflect profound compassion and acceptance.

As they draw nearer, they begin to speak. Listen to their comforting words, spoken in a tone filled with kindness and reassurance. They begin by saying, "I know you're disappointed in yourself. It's alright. We all make mistakes. We all have moments we wish we could do over. But these moments don't define you. They don't describe who you are."

Their words flow over you like a soothing balm, healing old wounds and easing the burdens you've carried. Your shoulders ease, your face relaxes, your whole body lets go of the tension it has been carrying.

They continue. "No one is perfect. And that makes us human. You need to be kind to yourself." They remind you that all these experiences make us who we are, and that growth often comes from the moments when we disappoint ourselves.

Feel them wrap you in a warm embrace. This is more than just a physical touch; they surround you with unconditional love and forgiveness. Allow yourself to lean in and feel the security and acceptance they offer. You stay in this embrace as long as you need.

When you step back, you feel their love and compassion surrounding you and slowly entering your heart. You smile.

They look into your eyes and say, "You are so loved and deserving of kindness, especially from yourself." They continue, "I'm always here for you. Whenever you need, I'll be in this clearing." They smile and then walk away, quickly disappearing.

You take a deep breath, inhaling the fresh air of the forest. You release any lingering feelings of shame, regret, or self-blame associated with that memory. The feelings dissipate into the air, leaving your heart lighter and freer.

Carrying their words and the warmth of their embrace in your heart, you continue your walk through the forest. With each step, you feel a renewed sense of acceptance of your beautifully imperfect journey through life.

Feel the solid earth beneath your feet, grounding you in your right to be just as you are. Continue walking through the forest, breathing deeply, feeling a sense of peace enveloping you. You are part of this beautiful world.

Carry these feelings with you as you return to your everyday life.

Meditation Journey Three: Walk on the Beach

Reflect on a recent moment when you felt disappointed in yourself. This moment will be a part of our upcoming journey.

Begin by finding a quiet, comfortable space where you can be undisturbed. Take a moment to settle in, feeling the support beneath you. Start by taking three long deep breaths. Exhale slowly with each breath. Allow yourself to be fully present in this moment, setting aside any worries and distractions.

Imagine standing on a vast ocean beach. The soft sand stretches out before you for miles, warm and velvety beneath your feet. Setting in the distance, the sun paints the sky in breathtaking shades of orange, pink, and purple. The horizon is a like an abstract painting, where the fiery orange blends seamlessly into soft pink, and then deepens into a rich, velvety purple as the sun sinks lower.

Beautiful colors dance on the water, infusing the waves with shades of deep purple and soft pink. Each wave catches the light differently, creating many colors that ripple and move like liquid art. The gentle lapping of the waves creates a soothing melody, and the salty breeze carries the faint scent of the ocean. The air is refreshing, and you breathe in it while you're immersed in the beauty of this moment.

You admire the sky with its streaks of vibrant pink and gold reflecting off the scattered clouds, making them look like fluffy, glowing cotton candy. Seagulls glide gracefully across this backdrop, their calls blending with the rhythmic sound of the waves. The entire scene fills you with a sense of peace and wonder.

You walk along the shoreline, feeling the gentle breeze against your skin. You listen to the rhythmic sound of the waves coming onto the shore and rolling back out. With each step, you feel calmer.

You notice the sand changing under the gentle wash of the waves. Its color and texture shift with each retreat, which reminds you of how life constantly changes. Every moment is transient, like the waves, teaching us that all situations, good or bad, eventually pass.

Now, think about a time when you disappointed yourself, when you felt let down by your actions. As you reflect on this memory, notice the emotions it stirs within you. Allow yourself to feel them fully, without judgment. Try to view that memory through a lens of kindness and understanding. Speak to yourself as you would to a cherished friend, reminding yourself that regrets are part of being human. We all make mistakes; you are no different from anyone else. There is no perfect person in this world, and mistakes are an inevitable part of life.

You feel the sand beneath your feet, noticing how it supports you. Let this sensation remind you that you are grounded on this earth. Now, imagine a warm, gentle light emanating from your heart. This light, a symbol of your inner compassion, spreads throughout your entire being. Watch as this light grows stronger, surrounding you with love, acceptance, and understanding. Let it envelop you, from the tips of your toes to the top of your head. This light reminds you constantly of the self-compassion within you that you can access at any time.

You reflect on your disappointment and recognize that you were doing the best you could at that time. You forgive yourself for what occurred, understanding that you were striving for happiness while responding to many challenges. While you regret what happened, you accept it.

As you are surrounded by this gentle, warm light, you realize this mistake belongs to the past and that it's time to look forward. Although you will bring along any lessons learned, the weight of regret must be left behind. Dwelling on past errors serves no purpose now. Instead, imagine this regret as footprints left in the wet sand— an imprint soon to be washed away by the waves. The ocean is vast and forgiving; it does not hold on to the shore. And you should not cling to past mistakes. Let the waves pull your burdens away, leaving behind a clean slate, smooth and unmarked, ready for new beginnings.

Walk along the beach, holding this self-compassion in your heart. Look back at your footprints behind you. Take a moment to really look at them. These footprints contain the harsh judgment you have placed on yourself. The ocean reaches the shore and slowly covers your footprints. With each visit to the shore, the waves cleanse the sand of your past, leaving nothing but a smooth, surface. And as you stride forward, your steps become lighter, unburdened by the weight that once clung to you. Each step frees you a little more.

When you look back, you no longer see the footprints. You see the vast beach in front of you, ready for you to put your prints there. The beach is a reminder of the endless possibilities ahead. And the rhythmic waves sing a soothing song of renewal. Let this sound of the water encourage you to move forward, to embrace each moment as a fresh opportunity. Feel hopeful about your future and the many steps ahead of you.

As you continue to walk on this beautiful beach, you take one last deep breath, savoring the peace and compassion you've nurtured within yourself during this journey. Remember, this beach is always here for you, a place you can return to whenever you need.

Hold on to these peaceful feelings as you slowly transition back to your current surroundings. Carry them with you as you go into your day or evening.

In the next chapters, I will explore self-compassion in specific areas of life.

- Chapter 1 is about embracing your body.
- Chapter 2 is about embracing personal relationships.
- Chapter 3 is about navigating stress and challenges.
- Chapter 4 is about embracing your financial journey.
- Chapter 5 is about embracing your physical and mental health.
- Chapter 6 is about embracing past mistakes.
- Chapter 7 is about embracing life transitions.
- Chapter 8 is about embracing your parenting journey.
- Chapter 9 is about navigating loss and grief.
- Chapter 10 is about healing from trauma.

- Chapter 11 is about embracing the experience of aging.
- The concluding chapter is about how to embrace self-kindness every day.

Chapter 1: Embracing Your Body

In a world increasingly focused on external appearances, it's no surprise that many of us struggle to accept our bodies. From a young age, we are bombarded with messages about how we should look, often leading to a constant battle with ourselves. Women, in particular, are judged harshly for their appearance, which can cause stress, anxiety, and conditions like bulimia or anorexia. However, the journey to body acceptance is not just about changing how we see ourselves in the mirror; it's about recognizing and honoring our bodies for the incredible marvels they truly are.

The human body is an intricate and sophisticated system, a masterpiece of biological engineering. Every second, millions of processes occur without our conscious effort—from the beating of our hearts to the intricate interactions of neurotransmitters in our brains. Our bodies carry us through life, adapting to challenges, healing from injuries, and enabling us to experience the world around us.

Yet, despite these remarkable capabilities, many of us focus on our perceived flaws in our appearance. We often forget the strength, resilience, and beauty inherent in our physical forms. This chapter aims to shift that perspective, guiding you towards a deeper appreciation of your body.

The Importance of Body Acceptance

Health and Well-Being: Accepting your body goes beyond aesthetics; it's fundamentally linked to your physical and mental health. Negative body image can lead to anxiety and depression. Feeling bad about one's body can also lead to behaviors that try to make us feel better, like binge eating and drinking, which only makes us feel worse.

Self-Esteem and Confidence: How we view our bodies significantly affects our overall self-esteem. Body acceptance fosters a stronger sense of self-worth and confidence.

Quality of Life: When we free ourselves from constant self-criticism about our bodies, we have more mental and emotional space to enjoy life and engage with the world more fully.

The Journey to Body Acceptance

Accepting one's body is deeply personal and often challenging. It involves changing the negative beliefs we have about our bodies and replacing them with a narrative of respect and gratitude. It's about seeing your body not as an enemy to be conquered or a project to be completed, but as an integral part of your unique human experience—deserving of care, love, and acceptance.

In this chapter, you will find meditations designed to help you cultivate a more positive relationship with your body. Remember, embracing your body doesn't mean you won't experience moments of self-doubt or discomfort. Nor does it imply that caring for your body's health or aiming for improvement is unnecessary. For example, if losing weight is part of your journey to better health, then pursue it. However, the core principle is not about change; it's about accepting and respecting your body for the crucial role it plays in your life. Recognize your body for what it is: an integral and beautiful part of who you are, encompassing both its strengths and vulnerabilities.

Meditation Journey Four: The Spa

Begin this meditation by finding a quiet and comfortable spot where you can sit undisturbed. Allow yourself the freedom to be present in this moment, away from the concerns of daily life. Take a deep, calming breath. As you exhale, feel any tension or stress leaving your body.

Imagine stepping through the doors of a unique spa, a sanctuary where every person's body is celebrated. This isn't just any spa. It's a haven of acceptance and appreciation. As you enter, the scents of jasmine and a hint of lavender fill the air, creating an atmosphere that calms your mind.

You're greeted by a guide, whose presence is as comforting as the environment. They lead you to a changing room, where you're provided with a soft, luxurious robe. Your guide directs you to a treatment room that overlooks a tranquil private garden. Natural light bathes the room, and the sound of a small fountain outside the window fills the air. You lie down on a bed that molds to your form, covered in soft linens.

Listening to the water bubbling through the fountain, you relax, sinking into the bed. As you enter a state of calmness, your guide enters the room. They reveal that each time they touch you, a soothing warmth will envelop you, instilling a sense of gratitude. This spa session will lead you to be thankful for every part of your body.

The guide's hands gently rest on your forehead, a light contact that sends a warmth through your entire body, relaxing you and creating a sense of gratitude. You suddenly recognize the miraculous nature of your body. You understand it has been your steadfast companion throughout life's journey, present in every moment and experience. Allow yourself to marvel at this realization, embracing a moment of profound appreciation for the extraordinary gift you have been given.

The guide's hands gently massage your head. In this moment, you silently feel gratitude for your scalp and hair. Your hair reflects vitality and is a unique part of your appearance. Your thoughts then shift to your brain, and you realize its incredible capabilities for thought, creativity, and the power of memory. It allows you to remember the beautiful moments of your life.

As your guide continues to massage your face, your attention turns to your eyes. Gratitude flows through you for the gift of sight, enabling you to absorb the beauty of the world, recognize the faces of those you cherish, and delight in the tapestry of colors around you. The guide's gentle touch near your ears prompts a deep appreciation for your ability to hear—the intricate layers of sounds, from music to laughter, to the voices of your loved ones, all enriching your world.

You become grateful for your nose and mouth—for the senses of smell and taste. You revel in the thought of the delightful flavors and scents they allow you to experience—chocolate, freshly baked bread, a rain-soaked earth, fragrant roses, and countless others. These senses enrich your life in so many ways, from the pleasure of tasting your favorite foods to the comfort of familiar scents. You feel grateful for your mouth to form words, enabling you to express thoughts, convey feelings, and connect with those around you.

The guide places their hands on your face and you appreciate its capacity for a wide range of expressions, allowing you to share joy, surprise, sadness, and a range of emotions, all without uttering a single word.

The guide's hands move to your neck and shoulders. Their touch warms and relaxes you, causing you to consider the heavy physical and emotional loads these parts of your body routinely bear. With each passing moment, you feel the weight of these burdens lift, allowing your neck and shoulders to release accumulated tension. This moment of release is a profound reminder of the resilience and support your body provides, even under the weight of life's challenges.

As the massage continues, the guide moves down to your arms and then to your hands. You relax these areas and feel gratitude. You think about how your arms embrace those you love, offering comfort and warmth. Your hands, capable of intricate tasks and tender gestures, allow you to create, to express, and to connect with the world. From making food, to creating a piece of art, to writing with a pen, hands make so many things possible.

You then focus on the center of your being—your chest and heart. A deep sense of thankfulness comes over you for the steady beat of your heart. This rhythm, so constant and reliable, is a reminder of the gift of life. You also consider your lungs expanding and contracting with each breath, a process so automatic yet miraculous, sustaining you moment by moment. You feel grateful for this central part of your body that allows you to live.

Next, the guide places their hands lightly on your stomach. You realize this part of you plays a crucial role in converting food into energy, fueling every cell, every thought, and every movement. You feel grateful for the silent, continuous work your stomach performs to support your health and well-being, your life's energy.

The massage then transitions, and the guide's hands make their way to your hips and legs. With each touch, you're reminded of the countless paths you've walked, the stability your legs have provided. You appreciate how your hips and legs have moved you along life's journey, for their role in movement and endurance.

Your guide now massages your feet. With every step, your feet connect you to the earth, reminding you of your place in the world and your connection to the earth. You feel grateful for this connection, so fundamental yet often overlooked, because it grounds and centers you.

Turning over, the guide's hands tenderly massage your back. You are thankful for its tremendous support and strength. You realize your back is crucial for standing and walking because it holds you upright, enabling you to face the world with confidence and purpose.

In these moments of reflection, you're filled with a deep appreciation for your body's complexity and its role in your existence. Now, in this state of gratitude, acknowledge any parts of your body you have viewed negatively. Take a moment to think about any part that you're critical of and offer it your gratitude. Say to it, "I appreciate your role in my life."

As the guide concludes the massage, they gently place their hands over your heart. They channel a warm, glowing light of gratitude directly into your heart space. This light feels as though it is igniting a flame within your very core that extends gratitude outwards to every part of your body. When you feel ready, return to your surroundings with a renewed sense of thankfulness and love for your body.

Meditation Journey Five: The Hall of Ancestors

Begin this meditation in a place where you can sit in comfort. Take three deep purposeful breaths, and with each one, feel any tension leaving your body.

Imagine stepping into the Hall of Ancestors, a place dedicated to your ancestral history. When you enter, the clamor and activity from the outside fade away, leaving behind a peaceful atmosphere. A long hallway stretches out in front of you, with many portraits on either side. The lighting here is soft, casting a gentle glow that gives everything a museum-like quality, yet the space feels welcoming.

As you walk through the Hall of Ancestors, you experience a combination of elegance and comfort. Portraits of your ancestors hang in gilded frames on the walls. Comfortable chairs are scattered throughout, inviting you to sit and reflect, making it easier to connect with the past in a relaxed setting.

You walk along the halls until you find several portraits of your parents. The images capture different times in their lives—when they were children, as they matured, and then as they married, and eventually, ones from their later years. You pause in front of each portrait, taking the time to appreciate the unique attributes of each parent.

Really look at them. Observe the fine lines etched on their faces, the sparkle in their eyes, the way their smiles change over the years. Notice the way they carried themselves, the subtle shift in their posture from youthful exuberance to the confidence of adulthood. You see the textures of their clothes, the styles changing with the eras, each detail telling a story of its own.

You take in the details that define them—from the warmth in their eyes to the curve of their lips, from the shape of their hands to the way they stood or sat. The expressions that cross their faces speak volumes of their experiences, their joys, their sorrows, and their love. Each portrait is a glimpse into their life.

Take a moment to contemplate these portraits of your parents. What physical traits do you recognize in yourself that mirror those of your parents? Look into a mirror nearby and see your own reflection. How does your face resemble theirs? In what ways does your body or your overall look resemble that of each parent? This moment is about understanding the physical connections that link you to your family.

Next, you visit the portraits of your grandparents. Take in the details of their features. The attire specific to their era, paying close attention to the different expressions captured in these portraits. Take a moment to discern the resemblances between your father and his parents—your grandparents. Look for the shared traits that bridge the generations. Then, turn your attention to your mother and her parents. Notice what they share in terms of appearance.

Now, consider the traits you've inherited from your parents and grandparents—the curve of your nose, the shape of your eyes, the texture of your hair, or the way your hands are formed. It could be the shape of your body, your height, or any distinctive physical quality. These features connect you directly to your parents and grandparents. These relatives embody countless stories and experiences, having lived lives filled with joy, sorrow, success, and adversity. Their love, losses, dreams, and struggles have woven a rich heritage that is uniquely yours. These physical resemblances are not random but are threads of connection to your ancestry.

Consider the ancestors you've never met but know through family stories. You visit these portraits that hang along the walls. Visualize how they looked, what they wore, and the expressions they carried through life. These were the people who embarked on significant journeys, perhaps emigrating to new countries with hopes for a better future. They found love, built families, and worked hard, facing and overcoming countless struggles along the way.

You realize your body isn't merely a collection of cells; it's a living testament to their perseverance, a tangible monument to your ancestors' enduring spirit. Each part of you carries a piece of their history, a testament to their lives, shaping who you are today.

Consider your unique features. Perhaps there's something about you that has always stood out. Reflect on this characteristic. The nose you thought was too big, too small, or not quite as you wanted.

It's actually a gift through time. It's a symbol of your family history. The color of your eyes, the shape of your smile, your skin tone, and the silhouette of your body—these are not accidental. They're direct links to your ancestors, a reflection of your shared lineage.

Feel a sense of pride as you think about these people. Your body is a living storybook of love, survival, and connection, carrying the wisdom, hopes, and dreams of those who came before you. It is the product of strong connections and the yearning to bring life into existence.

In this moment, embrace the beauty of your heritage. Each trait is a badge of honor, a physical manifestation of the love and struggles that have paved the way for you. Your body tells a story of resilience and continuity, a living legacy that connects you to your roots. Let this awareness fill you with gratitude and strength, knowing you are a part of something much larger than yourself. You are a bridge between the past and the future, carrying forward the essence of those who have shaped your existence.

As you contemplate this, allow feelings of love and respect to fill you. Your body deserves care and kindness, not just for what it does, but for what it represents. It's a living testament to the lives and loves of those who came before you.

Now, it's time to leave the Hall of Ancestors. When you feel ready, return to your current surroundings with a renewed sense of appreciation for your body and its ancestral beauty.

Meditation Journey Six: Magic Mirror

Begin this meditation in a peaceful, comfortable spot where you will not be disturbed. Sit down, gently close your eyes, and take a moment to settle into your space. Take three deep breaths, inhaling slowly and fully, then exhaling gently. With each breath, feel lighter and more relaxed.

Now, imagine you are in a serene, dimly lit room with soft, ambient music playing in the background. The slow, relaxing music causes you to breathe deeply. In this room stands a unique floor-to-ceiling mirror with a heavily gilded, ornate frame. You admire this large mirror and notice that it seems to display a few colors, as if showing you something special. It turns out this isn't an ordinary mirror—it's a magical one that reflects you at your best. It captures those moments when you truly felt and looked fabulous. The times when you were most attractive, when you looked great. Perhaps it was when you dressed up for a special event, or those ordinary days when everything just felt right.

As you stand before this remarkable mirror, it displays a series of images from your life. Each image is a snapshot of a time when you felt and looked genuinely attractive. Perhaps it was at a wedding or special event, or maybe when you went out to a restaurant, or even just on a day when you looked your best and felt great. Seeing yourself like this, at your peak, brings a warm, joyful smile to your face. It's a powerful reminder of how well you can feel about yourself, reflecting those times when you were most comfortable in your own skin and knew you looked good.

Watch as the mirror cycles through these images. What do you see reflected in these moments? Maybe it's the way your eyes light up when you laugh, or the poised way you carry yourself when you feel strong and capable. With each image, think about how you felt at the time.

Now, the mirror asks you to look deeper at the images of you when you were most attractive. Notice that when you see yourself happy, your attractiveness shines brighter. Happiness radiates from within, enhancing your features and making you glow. It's infectious, and it makes you more approachable, more beautiful.

In the images where you look confident, notice how your posture is straighter, your head held higher. Confidence amplifies your attractiveness by showing you believe in yourself. It's an aura that says you are comfortable in your own skin.

In moments where you feel valued and loved, your expression is open, content, fulfilled. Feeling valued boosts your self-esteem, which enhances your attractiveness. It's not just in your perception—others see and respond to this self-assured version of you.

Take a moment to reflect on these observations. Realize that being attractive isn't tied to conventional standards—it's not about weight, flawless skin, or perfect features. True attractiveness stems from how you feel about yourself. It's about the joy, confidence, and value you feel and express.

Now, as you continue to gaze into this magical mirror, notice a subtle but significant shift in its surface. The images from the past fade away, and the mirror now reflects your current self. However, this reflection is not just a simple mirror image. It shows you embodying all the confidence, happiness, and sense of value that you've observed in your past selves.

Look closely. See yourself standing there, your posture poised and confident. Your eyes sparkle with a deep, inner joy. The corners of your mouth turn upwards in a gentle, contented smile. This is you, as you are now, infused with all the positive attributes you've admired in your earlier reflections.

Allow yourself to really feel these qualities intensifying within you. With each breath, confidence builds, happiness blooms, and your sense of self-worth solidifies. These feelings are not just fleeting; they are part of who you are.

As you embody these traits, imagine how others respond to this vibrancy. Visualize the people in your life—friends, family, colleagues—seeing this version of you. Notice their smiles as they interact with you, the warmth in their eyes, the open, appreciative gestures they make. They are responding not just to your outward appearance, but to your energy and spirit.

Now, extend this visualization further. Imagine strangers you pass by on the street, or people you meet in daily activities, reacting to this confident, happy version of yourself. They also sense your self-assured, joyful presence. Their reactions are positive, reinforcing your own feelings of self-worth and attractiveness.

As you stand before the mirror, observe this wonderful cycle: the more you radiate these inner qualities, the more they are reflected back to you by the world. The more you expect the world to like you, the happier and more attractive you become. The better you feel about yourself, the more attractive you appear. Like a beautiful echo, the positivity you emit returns to you, amplified by the interactions and relationships you engage in.

Feel this connection deeply. It is profound and real. Understand that your thoughts and feelings about yourself shape how the world sees and treats you. By holding yourself in a positive light, by truly feeling and believing in your own value and beauty, you influence the world around you. This is the power of your own perception. Your view of yourself becomes your reality.

Hold this vision for a few more moments. With each breath, let these feelings of attractiveness, confidence, and worth grow stronger. You are not just imagining this; you are allowing your true self to be seen and appreciated, both by yourself and by others.

Take a few moments to really anchor this experience. Feel the joy and the empowerment that comes from knowing you can shape your own reality through self-compassion and self-confidence. When you are ready, gently bring your attention back to your current environment, carrying with you this renewed sense of self with you, knowing that your true beauty is reflected not just in a mirror, but in every moment of your life when you choose to see it.

Chapter 2: Embracing Personal Relationships

One of the most crucial and often challenging aspects of our lives is our personal relationships. Whether these are friendships, romantic relationships or ones with family, they are fundamental to our emotional well-being and life satisfaction. Yet, they are far from simple. They require effort, understanding, and often, a great deal of patience.

In personal relationships, gratitude, empathy, and forgiveness play a vital role. These elements are not just emotional responses, but foundational pillars that uphold and enrich our connections with others. Understanding and cultivating these practices can transform our connections into sources of deep fulfillment and growth.

Gratitude creates more positive relationships because it helps us appreciate the value of these connections. By fostering a sense of thankfulness for the people in our lives and the moments we share with them, we cultivate a relationship where appreciation and mutual respect flourish. Gratitude encourages us to focus on the abundance in our relationships, rather than what might be lacking, promoting a stronger bond with our loved ones.

Empathy, or the capacity to understand and share the feelings of another, is the cornerstone of successful relationships. It enables us to see the world through the eyes of others, to feel what they feel, and to respond with genuine understanding. Empathy paves the way for better emotional connections, where individuals feel seen, heard, and valued. It is through empathy that we can navigate the complexities of others' emotions, building stronger relationships.

Forgiveness is the balm that heals the inevitable wounds inflicted by misunderstandings, disagreements, and hurtful actions. Challenges are inevitable in meaningful relationships, and forgiveness is key to preserving strong bonds. Forgiveness allows us to release the burdens of resentment and anger that can weigh heavily and cause a disintegration in the connection. Through forgiveness, we open the door to reconciliation and healing, enabling our relationships to recover and grow stronger. Forgiveness does not erase the past but allows us to embrace the present and future with an open heart, free from the pain of past grievances.

In this chapter, the meditations journeys can help you integrate gratitude, empathy, and forgiveness into your relationships. By doing so, you will support and uplift those you love.

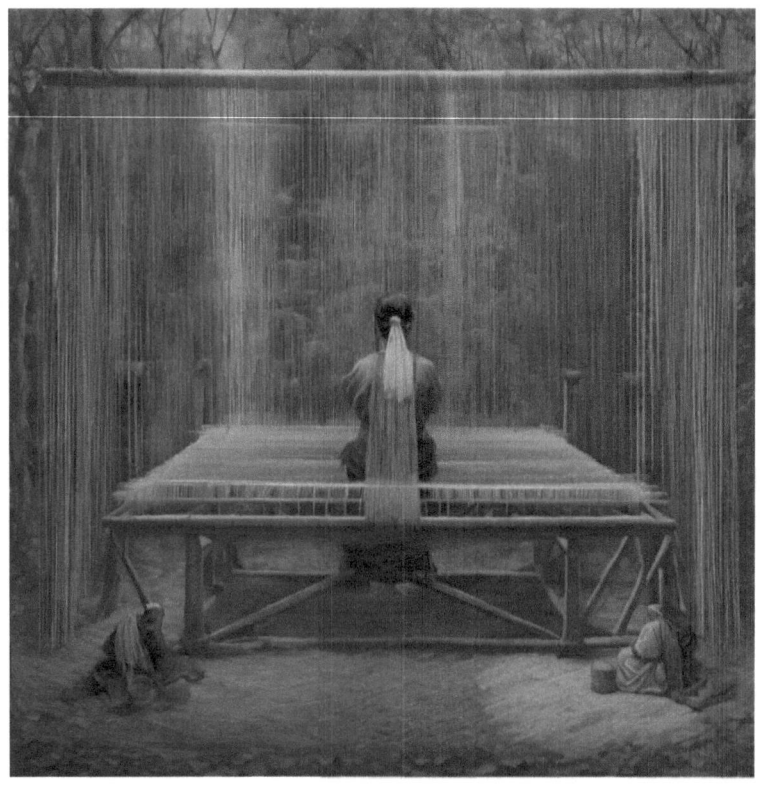

Meditation Journey Seven: Deepening Gratitude at Weaver's Grove

Find a comfortable space where you can sit undisturbed. Begin by focusing on your breath, inhaling deeply to invite peace into your heart. Exhale slowly to release any tension. With each breath, allow yourself to drift into a deeper state of relaxation.

Imagine walking down a forest path covered in a light mist. This path leads you to a special place known as the Weaver's Grove, a mystical clearing that feels removed from the rest of the world.

In the center of this grove stands an ancient tree, its branches sprawling skyward, with roots anchored deeply in the earth. Under this tree you find the Weaver of Lives, a figure seated at a large, intricate loom with their back to you. This loom is not ordinary. Its threads of many colors seem to glow gently.

The grove is quiet. The only sounds are the soft rustling of the tree leaves and a faint, comforting background hum of the sounds of nature. There is a subtle light that makes everything seem more vivid. As you breathe in the fresh air, a feeling of calm envelops you.

You approach the weaver, noticing their peacefulness. The weaver looks up with a gentle smile, their eyes reflecting a deep wisdom. They gesture towards a seat next to the loom, welcoming you to sit and watch them weave.

As you settle in, the weaver explains the significance of the textile on the loom. "Each thread and color you see represents the various relationships that have shaped who you are. Like this tapestry, your life is a complex, interconnected web of influences and bonds."

First, the weaver selects threads of gold and silver, representing the current connections that bring joy into your life. Perhaps this is a partner, close family member, or dear friend. Take a moment to visualize this person. See their face and imagine your love in the form of a white light coming from you to them. Now think of another person with whom you have a wonderful relationship. See their face and also send love to them in the form of a white light. As you do so, the weaver threads these gold colors into the tapestry.

Then, the weaver chooses dark-blue threads, which symbolize your earliest relationships. You think of a family member or childhood friend who was important to you. Picture their face, recall their voice, and remember a moment you shared. Think about this time and what this person did for you. Hold on to this memory. What lessons did this relationship teach you about love? What did you learn about the world from this person? Now, allow feelings of gratitude to wash over you for the role this person played in your life. The weaver places these dark-blue threads carefully into the tapestry.

Next, a vibrant yellow thread catches the weaver's attention, symbolizing a friendship that has significantly shaped you. Perhaps this is a friend from school or a person who has been by your side through various phases of life. Think about this person—visualize them in your mind. Reflect on a specific instance that strengthened your bond. What did you learn from this person? What did you gain from this relationship? Recall some major memories of them. As this yellow thread is woven into the tapestry, feel your heart swell with gratitude for this connection.

The loom glows with a soft, pulsating light as the weaver introduces a thread of deep crimson, representing a romantic relationship that holds a special place in your heart. Whether it's a current partner or a past love. Think about this person. Visualize them and think of a significant memory. Acknowledge both the joys and challenges you've experienced with them. Now consider how they've contributed to your growth as a person. Send love and gratitude to this individual, cherishing the role they've played in your life journey. The weaver threads this deep crimson strand into the tapestry.

Now they select a thread with a green shade, symbolizing a challenging relationship. Contemplate a connection that has tested you—perhaps a family member with whom you've had differences, a friend who drifted away, or someone you've clashed with. Try to view this relationship in terms of what it has given you. What lessons have you learned from this person? Think of this individual and extend gratitude for these valuable life lessons, recognizing their contribution to your growth.

Finally, the weaver incorporates a thread of light blue, representing relationships that have ended or transformed. Visualize a person with whom you no longer have a relationship and think about a significant memory you have of them. Consider what this relationship gave you. Honor the space this connection once held in your life. Remember the joy it brought you. Send peaceful thoughts towards this person, appreciating the part they've played in your story. The weaver puts this light-blue thread into the textile.

As your tapestry takes shape, you feel a profound sense of gratitude for the many relationships that have been a part of your life. From happy relationships to more challenging ones, each has added to your journey and has taught you something.

Take a deep breath and think about all these relationships. Bring to mind anyone else that is important to you and watch the weaver put those threads into the piece in front of you. It could be a good friend, a person who helps you, a professional, a neighbor, an old love, or someone you see regularly whom you don't know well. It could be someone from your past who has had a profound impact on you. Take a moment to send them light and gratitude for their role in your life.

Now it's time to leave Weaver's Grove. When you're ready, gently return to your current environment, carrying with you a renewed appreciation for the intricate tapestry of your life's connections.

Meditation Journey Eight: Garden of Empathy

Find a quiet space where you can sit comfortably. Begin by taking a few deep breaths. Inhale deeply, filling your lungs, and exhale slowly, letting go of any tension or stress. Take several additional deep breaths and allow your shoulders to drop while you let your body sink into the surface where you're sitting.

As you continue to breathe slowly and deeply, turn your attention to the idea of empathy, which is the ability to understand and share the feelings of another person. It plays a powerful role in building connections and fostering understanding.

Imagine you are entering the Garden of Empathy, which fosters introspection and understanding. The fragrance of blooming flowers and rich earth fills the air, inviting you to take deep, cleansing breaths. You smell the scent of roses and freshly turned soil.

You appreciate the gentle rustle of leaves, the subtle hum of bees busily working, and the soft chirping of birds hidden in the foliage. Around you, the garden is alive with color and life. A cluster of wildflowers dances in the breeze to your left, their vibrant blue petals—contrasting beautifully with the lush green grass.

The paths in front of you curve gently through the garden and are laid with smooth stones. Each path offers benches along the way, sturdy yet elegant, made of polished wood. These benches are thoughtfully placed, providing inviting spaces to pause, sit, and reflect.

You find a bench near some emerald-colored bushes. As you sit, surrounded by the beauty and tranquility of the garden, you feel a profound sense of calm enveloping you, preparing your heart and mind to be empathetic. You breathe in the crisp, scented air and enjoy the sight of pink roses to your left along the pathway.

As you sit, someone you care deeply about enters the garden from another location and walks towards you along one path. This is a person you know well. As they come closer, you notice their expressions, their smile, and hear them greet you. A special moment you shared with them comes to mind as they approach. Observe their posture, their demeanor, and how they carry themselves.

You smile at this person and then rise to walk alongside them on the garden path. The sun filters through the leaves, casting shadows on the ground as you stroll together. You engage in some small talk, commenting on the beauty of the garden and the pleasant weather. Slowly, the conversation deepens as they tell you about some frustrations they're having in their life. They then share their deepest desires and current challenges. You listen closely.

Thinking about their current challenges, you imagine what it would feel like to be in their position. How would these difficulties impact you? Perhaps you don't always consider these things when you interact with this person. You recall the many things you know about them—their past, the hardships they have overcome, and the disappointments they have faced.

You tell them you appreciate their situation and empathize with their current struggles, explaining that you hope they feel supported and valued by you. They are not alone on their journey. You offer words of encouragement, assuring them you understand their struggles and that you are here for them, ready to listen or help whenever they need it.

You feel a sense of empathy for them, which manifests as a warm, golden light emanating from your heart, enveloping them completely. This light symbolizes your understanding of their current struggles. See this light flowing into their heart, conveying your understanding and your desire for their happiness. Picture this light soothing them, offering a feeling of peace.

Now, you send this person into the garden, giving them a comforting hug before they depart. As they walk away, you continue to visualize the golden light surrounding them, providing a sense of peace and comfort. You feel a profound connection with them, knowing that your empathy has created an understanding between you both.

Now, gently shift your focus to someone else who can benefit from your compassion. This person is someone you know who also enters the garden, approaching you along a winding path. You think about them and recall a particular interaction from the past. As they approach, you notice their expression and body language. See them greet you as you acknowledge their presence in this shared, peaceful space.

You walk alongside them in the garden. They tell you hesitantly about some challenges they are facing in their lives. They reveal their current problems and some of their worries and frustrations. You consider how their struggles may influence their behavior towards you and others. You realize they are doing the best they can, even if it's not what you would do.

As you walk by some fragrant flowers, they tell you about their dreams and what they want in both the short term and the long term. Perhaps they say they want to be happy, healthy, financially stable, or loved. Try to connect with their desires from a place of compassion.

You walk alongside them and tell them you have a deeper understanding of them, their hopes, and their struggles. You send understanding to them in the form of a warm, golden light flowing from you and surrounding them completely. This light represents your empathy. Visualize this light flowing into their heart, conveying your understanding and your desire for their happiness. Picture this light soothing them, offering reassurance. Now, you send this person into the garden, giving them a handshake or comforting hug before they leave.

You continue to walk through the Garden of Empathy and encounter anyone who needs kindness in your current life. Walking with them, you gain a perspective on their desires and struggles. You surround them with your golden light and then send them along their way.

Now it's time to leave the garden. When you're ready, come back to your current environment, carrying with you a renewed dedication for compassion in all your relationships.

Meditation Journey Nine: Bridge to Forgiveness

Find a quiet place where you can sit comfortably. Bring your awareness to your breath. Take a deep breath in, filling your lungs completely, and then slowly exhale, feeling more relaxed with each breath. Feel the support of the ground beneath you, offering a sense of stability. With every inhalation, draw in calmness and peace. With every exhalation, let go of any tension or stress.

Imagine you are standing at the edge of a tranquil river. The waters gently flow along, creating a soothing melody. Observe how the river carries away fallen leaves, each leaf a symbol of past grievances and prior pains being softly sent away. The water sparkles under the warm sunlight, casting shimmering reflections on the surface.

An ancient, beautifully crafted bridge crosses over this river. This stone bridge is more than a structure; it's a mystical passage built to connect two realms—the shores of hurt where you've lingered, and the land of forgiveness that awaits your arrival. The bridge is adorned with intricate carvings of vines and flowers, worn smooth by centuries of weather and time. Birds chirp softly in nearby trees, their songs filling the peaceful surroundings. You take a deep breath, inhaling the fresh air, and feel a sense of calm wash over you.

Think about someone you wish to forgive and a specific thing you want to forgive them for. As you hold their image in your mind, observe any emotions that surface, recognizing them without judgment. Are you feeling anger, sadness, or perhaps disappointment? Acknowledge these emotions as they are, without trying to suppress or change them. They are a valid and natural part of your experience.

Now, reflect on the situation that led to these feelings. What exactly happened? Revisit the events with as much clarity as possible. Picture the setting, the words exchanged, and the actions taken. How did it unfold, and what were the key moments that caused your pain? Allow yourself to fully understand your own perspective and the impact it had on you.

You take a deep breath, feeling the cool air fill your lungs, and try to see the situation from the other person's perspective. Imagine stepping into their shoes, seeing the world through their eyes. What might they have been feeling or thinking? Even though they hurt you, is it possible they were not acting out of malice or unkindness? Reflect on their life, their struggles, and their experiences.

Consider that perhaps they did not see the situation as fully as you did. Could it be that their own fears, insecurities, or misunderstandings clouded their vision? Is it possible they did not realize how much this would affect you? Were they in a great deal of emotional or physical pain? As you ponder these questions, notice if there are any shifts in your emotional landscape.

Take a moment to recognize that they are human, just like you, and capable of making mistakes. They have their own vulnerabilities and limitations. Perhaps they were dealing with their own problems or confusion, which influenced their actions. Acknowledge that being human means being imperfect and can lead to hurting others.

As you hold this understanding, allow yourself to feel compassion for them. This does not mean excusing their behavior or diminishing your own feelings. It simply means recognizing their humanity and the complexity of their situation.

Consider the impact that holding onto this resentment has had on you. Has it brought you peace or has it been a burden? Often, forgiveness is not just about freeing the other person from their mistake. It's about freeing yourself from the weight of carrying that pain.

Imagine this hurt you've been carrying is a heavy object. Like a big rock or some other cumbersome item. Feel its weight in your hands, the strain it puts on your arms, and the tension it creates in your body. When you're ready, set this object down on the side of the river. As you put it on the ground, notice the way your muscles relax and the tension eases. Feel the lightness and the relief spreading through your entire being. This act is a symbol of your willingness to let go of the pain and move forward. It does not mean that what happened was okay, but it means that you choose not to let it control your emotions and peace of mind anymore.

Now, turn your attention to the bridge before you. It stretches across the sapphire river, inviting you to embark on a journey towards healing. You slowly begin to walk across it, each step a deliberate move towards forgiveness. The bridge, with its sturdy structure and ancient stonework, provides a passage from the pain of the past towards a future with greater peace.

As you walk, you touch the sides of the bridge and feel the texture of the rough stone under your fingertips. The air is cool and crisp, carrying the fresh scent of water and earth. As you watch, the river below effortlessly glides by carrying several twigs and leaves downstream. This water is a reminder of life's continual movement and the possibility of renewal.

Halfway across the bridge, you pause and take a deep breath. You are at the midpoint between hurt and forgiveness, and it's okay to take this journey at your own pace. Look back and see the hurt that you left on the other side of the river. Look forward and see the forgiveness. Think about what it will be like not to carry this burden any longer. Now say the following things to yourself.

"I forgive you for what you have done. I do not agree with your actions, but I forgive you."

"I release the past and open my heart to the present."

"Forgiving is my choice, and it brings me closer to peace."

Feel the strength of your compassion and the peace that comes with it. Forgiveness is a path you walk, a choice that leads you to peace and healing.

When you're ready, continue walking to the other side of the bridge. As you reach the bank, you feel a sense of release. You are no longer carrying this heavy weight. You have chosen the path of forgiveness, which is a powerful act of compassion for you and for the other person.

Now it's time to come back to the present moment, carrying this feeling into your day or evening.

Chapter 3: Navigating Stress and Challenges

Stress is an inescapable part of life. If you care deeply about something, whether it's your work, relationships, personal goals, or even your own well-being, it's likely to cause you stress at some point. But it's important to recognize that stress and challenges are deeply intertwined. Stress isn't just a side effect of the obstacles we face. Instead, it's a reflection of our commitment to what truly matters to us. It springs from the worry that we might not be able to navigate the challenges that come our way, casting a shadow of doubt over our abilities.

In today's fast-paced existence, we're often swept into a maelstrom of responsibilities and expectations. This constant juggling act, striving to keep all our plates spinning, amplifies our stress, making each challenge seem impossible. The crux of our stress often lies in a fear of inadequacy—worrying that we're not living up to our own standards or those set by others, and dreading the moment everything comes crashing down.

Recognizing this stress is a crucial first step towards managing it. Ironically, the reason for much of our stress is a lack of self-compassion. We set high expectations for ourselves, often judge ourselves for falling short, and overlook the importance of self-care. Relentless self-criticism can lock us in a vicious cycle, making stress seem like an insurmountable foe.

However, viewing stress through the lens of self-compassion reveals its dual nature: stress is both an obstacle and an opportunity for growth. It indicates our deep investment in aspects of our lives and can motivate us to reflect on our priorities, values, and limits.

Embracing stress with kindness and understanding towards ourselves allows us to transform our relationship with it, guiding us towards healthier responses and, ultimately, personal growth.

Stress also arises when we encounter challenging situations. These challenges are not signs of inadequacy but are instead opportunities for us. Complex problems are not easily solved, and overcoming obstacles takes time. This is a natural part of life. By cultivating self-compassion, we create a nurturing inner environment that empowers us to meet challenges with courage and resilience, replacing self-criticism with encouragement and judgment with empathy.

The meditation journeys in this chapter will help you cultivate patience and self-compassion during stressful times.

Meditation Journey Ten: The Compassionate Cabin

Begin by finding a quiet, comfortable space where you can relax and will not be distracted. Allow yourself a few moments to settle into this space, feeling the weight of your body supported. Take a deep, slow breath in, filling your lungs with air, and then gently release it, letting go of any tension or thoughts that are crowding your mind. Repeat this breathing pattern a few more times to fully relax.

Imagine walking toward a tranquil wood cabin, nestled within the forest where towering pines stand around it. This cabin is a special place where visitors are surrounded by a compassionate energy that helps them see all challenges through a lens of understanding. Here, issues become less daunting and more manageable.

The air in the woods is fragrant with pine and the subtle, earthy scent of the forest floor, freshly dampened by a recent rain. You step onto the porch of this cabin where a few chairs and a small, handcrafted table invite you to pause and relax. The dark green door proudly displays a welcome sign, and a note assures you that the cabin is unlocked, welcoming you by name.

Stepping through the creaky wooden door, you admire the rustic walls and the charming, mismatched furniture. The softness of woven rugs balances the roughness of the wooden floors, and the walls showcase stunning photographs of snow-capped mountains, majestic trees, and fields of wildflowers. A single photo catches your eye—a colorful lake at sunset. There seem to be phrases underneath each picture, but you're too far away to read them. On the other side of the room, bookshelves crammed with several worn books invite you to lose yourself in tales that vary from romance to adventure.

The air inside feels different. Lighter and imbued with a comforting energy. It wraps around you and makes you feel calmer.

You settle into a plush, inviting chair upholstered in soft, red plaid fabric. It's positioned perfectly to allow a view of the wilderness beyond the cabin's expansive windows. The chair's deep cushions support you, offering a comfortable place to take the weight of the world from your shoulders.

You relish this sanctuary. Here, in this secluded haven, time slows, and for a while, you can indulge in the luxury of simply being. Sinking deeper into your comfortable chair, you relax and breathe deeply.

You think about a current challenge you are facing. It could be a situation at work, a personal relationship difficulty, a health concern, or anything that you find tough right now. This could be a new or an old issue. As you think about this issue, acknowledge all the feelings associated with it. Notice if there's fear, frustration, anger, sadness, or any other emotions.

Observe these feelings without judgment, simply allowing them to be. These feelings are a normal reaction to life's difficulties. They are indicators of your engagement and your humanity. In this safe, cozy cabin, you fully embrace these emotions, understanding that they don't define you, but are simply a part of your current journey.

You take a deep breath, allowing the cabin's subtle, compassionate energy to fill you. As you exhale, you realize how important it is to show kindness to yourself, acknowledging that navigating issues is difficult. Your emotions and your current challenge are interconnected, each influencing the other. The stress from your challenge can amplify your emotions, making them feel more intense, while your emotional state can affect how you perceive and handle a challenge. Recognizing this connection helps you approach the situation with greater self-awareness and compassion. This moment of reflection helps you understand that embracing these emotions with compassion is a crucial step toward managing your challenges more effectively.

You wander through the cabin, admiring each landscape picture on the walls. Beneath the picture of the snow-capped mountains, a phrase reads, "Each peak I conquer builds my strength." Below the image of the majestic trees, it says, "I nurture my inner peace, growing steady and strong like these enduring trees." And as you step over to the picture of fields of wildflowers, you find the words, "I allow myself the space to heal and bloom in my own time."

As you ponder these phrases, you realize difficulties come and go. Life is always changing. Much like nature, which endures and adapts through the seasons, you too, have an innate resilience and capacity for growth. As you stand before the picture of the lake at sunset, you see the words, "I am more than my challenges."

Think of the support systems you have in place—the friends and family or even your inner resources you've cultivated over time. Feel grateful for this support, recognizing how important it is in your journey.

You remind yourself that difficulties are an integral part of life. They are not a reflection of your worth or capabilities, but opportunities for growth and learning. And you say to yourself, "I am doing the best I can with the knowledge and resources I have. It's okay to find this hard. It's okay to feel what I'm feeling."

Reflecting on your journey, you realize that every challenge has brought you valuable lessons, shaping you into a stronger, more resilient person. You have faced many challenges before, and you have grown as a result. As you consider your current issue, you say, "I see you. I feel you. But I am more than you. With self-compassion and resilience, I will navigate through you." You acknowledge that this moment, like all others, will pass, and you will emerge wiser and more capable, ready to embrace whatever comes next.

You step outside the cabin, feeling that you can address your current challenge. Now it's time to come back to your current environment, carrying the sense of self-compassion into your day or evening.

Meditation Journey Eleven: Navigating the Cobblestone Road

Find a tranquil space where you can sit undisturbed. Choose a spot that feels safe and comforting, whether it's a cozy corner of your home or a peaceful outdoor setting. Settle into a comfortable position and take a deep, cleansing breath. With each exhale, feel your shoulders drop and release any tension. Close your eyes and focus on the rhythm of your breath, allowing your mind to quiet. Inhale slowly and hold your breath. Then exhale slowly. As you continue to breathe deeply, feel yourself sinking deeper into a state of relaxation.

Imagine standing on a cobblestone road at dawn, a symbol of your life's journey unfolding before you. The road stretches out ahead, lined with trees and flanked by meadows, forests, and rivers. The cobblestones are uneven, varying in size, with some large stones pitted, broken, or even missing in places. Despite its imperfections, the road invites you to walk along it. You pause for a moment, feeling the steady support of the stones beneath your feet.

This cobblestone road mirrors your life. Along the way, there are patches where the stones are rough and uneven, symbolizing challenges, such as financial worries, health concerns, or relationship issues. Conversely, you will find other areas worn smooth, representing the easier periods of your existence. However, no road is entirely smooth for anyone. We all encounter rough patches on our journey.

Looking back, you see parts of the road that were tough, where the road was uneven or nonexistent. These were the difficulties you faced. Yet, you got past them. Think about some of the hardest times of your life. Consider how you managed these challenges, perhaps not perfectly, but you did the best you could. And you rose to these challenges. Take a moment to realize that you have been stronger and more resilient than you expected. Think about all the things you've been through—how you've survived and possibly thrived. Gently smile and feel proud of all the stressful things you managed.

Turning forward, you walk down the cobblestone road. There are spots where stones have shifted or are uneven and it's difficult to get your footing. Despite this, the road continues, framed by trees and dappled sunlight on the ground—a reminder that beauty often occurs within imperfections.

You think about a particular source of stress you are currently facing. Visualize it and imagine how this stress manifests on your cobblestone road. It might appear as a cluster of stones jutting out, an area where the road seems washed away, or where a stream cuts across your path. Name this stress and see its representation on the road. Notice the impact of this stress on your body. The tension it creates, the emotional responses it triggers. Allow yourself to sit with these feelings, acknowledging their presence without judgment. You are here on this path, and these feelings are part of life. It's part of being human.

You speak to yourself with words of comfort and reassurance, "This stress is part of my journey. It shows how much I care. I can see how the path ahead is difficult. But I can manage it. I am not stuck."

You consider any fears you're experiencing. Looking at these fears realistically, you ask yourself, "What is the worst that could happen? How likely is it that the most awful thing will actually occur?" Even if that possibility were to unfold, you know you have the resilience and the strength to continue along this road.

At this moment, you recognize you can manage and say, "I am doing my best. I can handle this challenge and this stress. I will approach myself with kindness and empathy."

Now, with a deep sense of self-compassion, you stand before the rough patch on your road. Take a moment to survey this challenging section with patience and understanding. Acknowledge the difficulties it represents and assert your ability to navigate through it. Feel a calm confidence rise within you as you prepare to cross. You know you can get across this difficult part of the road. You've done it before, and you will do it again.

Consider all the small and large actions you will take to alleviate this stress and deal with this challenge. Moving forward, you slowly and carefully navigate this part of the road. With each step, you are mindful of where you place your feet, taking your time to ensure each move is thoughtful and steady. If you stumble or fall, you gently pick yourself up and offer a compassionate reminder: "This is difficult. It will take time, and I may make mistakes, but everyone falls, and everyone makes mistakes." This careful and compassionate approach not only helps you find the best path through the obstacles but also teaches you to be kind to yourself throughout the journey. You consider your current stressful situation and how you will navigate it—with kindness, with patience, and with the belief that you can traverse difficult terrain.

With self-compassion, you give yourself the space to handle challenges without rushing or being harsh toward yourself. This mindful approach not only helps you cross the current rough patch, but also equips you with the resilience to face future hurdles on your journey.

You navigate your way across the hard part of the road. It takes some time, but you manage to do it. Look ahead and realize there will be additional tough stretches on your path. But just as you've done before, you will traverse these. The rough patches are not insurmountable. And within you lies the power to soften the hard edges of life.

Take a few deep breaths, letting this realization deepen. You say to yourself, "I have the strength and the kindness to find my way on this road. My compassion will help me along the way."

You look ahead and watch the sun climbing higher, brightening the sky. You realize you have all you need to traverse this journey. Now, come back to your present environment and bring these thoughts and feelings into your day or evening.

Meditation Journey Twelve: Discovering Wisdom Within a Magical Castle

Begin by finding a comfortable and quiet place where you can sit. Close your eyes and take a few deep, slow breaths to center yourself. With each inhale, draw in peace and calm; with each exhale, release any discomfort you might be holding. Let your body relax more deeply with every breath, feeling supported and safe.

Now, imagine yourself walking along a winding path through a mystical forest. The surrounding trees are ancient and wise, their leaves whispering secrets. A gentle light fills the air, casting a soft glow on the path ahead. You feel a sense of curiosity and anticipation as you walk, guided by an inner pull towards something significant.

You come upon a majestic castle atop a small hill. Its stone walls, aged and weathered, rise to impressive heights. As you draw closer, you notice the towering spires with slate roofs glistening in the light, with pennants fluttering at their tips. The structure is expansive, sprawling over a wide area, suggesting many rooms and hallways within.

The castle's architecture blends Gothic and medieval styles, with pointed arches, ribbed vaults, and flying buttresses. As you walk along the path, you see turrets interwoven with ivy, and friendly gargoyles perched on ledges, their shadows giving them an almost lifelike appearance. Warm light pours from the castle's many windows, hinting at richly furnished rooms and cozy spaces within. Balconies with wrought-iron railings, entwined with climbing roses, offer views of the surrounding landscape, adding to the castle's enchantment.

Finally, you reach the main entrance, an arched doorway flanked by torch-lit sconces that beckon you inside. Above the entrance, a large stained-glass window depicts legendary heroes and heroines in vibrant colors, surrounded by intricate carvings of mythical creatures and ancient symbols. The overall impression is one of timeless beauty and enchantment.

As you get closer, the large mahogany door opens, as if by magic, inviting you inside. As you step into the castle, you find yourself in a grand hall with vaulted ceilings, the air filled with the subtle scent of aged wood and a hint of lavender. The hall exudes an aura of timeless elegance and serenity. A long hallway extends from the grand hall, adorned with plush red carpets that create an elegant pathway. You can't help but feel that something wonderful is about to happen.

You walk through the hall, feeling a magnetic pull towards a particular room. Trusting your intuition, you arrive at a large wooden door that seems destined for you. With a deep breath, you open it. Soft, golden light filters through tall, arched stained glass windows in the room, creating a colorful display on the floors and walls.

In the center of the room, seated on an ornate throne, is a figure radiating wisdom and compassion. You recognize this figure as a wiser, more enlightened version of yourself, or perhaps a wise being who embodies the qualities you aspire to. They could be an older person or a younger one, yet their presence feels timeless. This luminous being smiles warmly, inviting you into the room, and says, "I have been expecting you."

You approach this figure with an open heart, ready to receive the wisdom they have to offer. They smile at you with understanding and kindness. You feel an immediate sense of peace and safety, knowing you are in the presence of profound wisdom. A plush armchair sits opposite this figure, and you take a seat.

You describe the challenge that has been weighing heavily on your heart. The fears that have been gnawing at you, the doubts that creep into your mind during quiet moments, and the many emotions that have stirred within you. You speak of your uncertainty, the worry that you are not enough, and the anxiety of potential failure. Recounting significant moments, you share everything that is on your mind. You reveal your most vulnerable thoughts and feelings.

The wise being listens attentively, their presence soothes your troubled spirit. As you pour out your heart, you feel a mixture of vulnerability and relief. When you have finished, they speak, their voice calm and clear. They remind you that every challenge carries within it the seeds of growth and learning. "Within every difficulty," they say, "lies an opportunity to discover your strength and resilience."

They continue by reminding you about the importance of being compassionate towards yourself. They say, "treat yourself with the same kindness and understanding you would offer to a dear friend or relative who is experiencing the same challenge."

As your conversation unfolds, the wise being shares some thoughts about your current issue, offering perspectives you hadn't considered. Their words shed some light on your situation. Listen to them closely and ask them any questions. Take a moment to hear what they have to say.

They also remind you that you have the wisdom that can guide you through any difficulty. "Within you lies a deep well of inner wisdom," they say softly. "You have cultivated this through all your experiences, your triumphs, and your trials. It is an intrinsic part of who you are. When you face challenges, it's easy to doubt yourself and feel overwhelmed, but remember that you have the knowledge and intuition to find your way. Trust in your inner voice, the quiet guidance that has led you through tough times before. Every answer you seek is already within you, waiting to be discovered."

Before you leave, the figure offers you a symbolic gift, a token of the insights you have gained. Accept this gift, holding it close to your heart, feeling its energy empowering and strengthening you.

You thank the wise being for their guidance, stand and make your way back to the grand hall, feeling lighter and more assured. As you exit the castle, you feel ready to face your challenge with a renewed sense of purpose and strength.

Now, come back to your present environment, taking this feeling into your day or evening.

Chapter 4: Embracing Your Financial Journey

In a world where success is often measured in monetary terms, the pressure to achieve financial stability and prosperity can be overwhelming. Financial pressure is a common experience for many people. From the pursuit of a higher income to the desire for material possessions, these financial goals can often become a central focus. Sadly, society often equates financial success with personal success, creating a culture where wealth is a key indicator of one's value and achievements. Sometimes, our focus on financial success can overshadow the significance of other areas in our lives, leading to stress and a skewed sense of self-worth. The pursuit of financial goals can also affect our mental and emotional well-being. Financial pressures can also strain personal relationships, becoming a source of conflict and tension.

It is important to learn to practice self-compassion in your financial life, understanding that your financial status does not define your worth as a person. Remember, your financial journey is just one part of your life's story. It's important to approach it with understanding and kindness, recognizing that true wealth comes from a life lived in alignment with your values and filled with meaningful experiences.

Although finances are an important aspect of life, they are not the sole determinant of happiness or success. My goal is to help you redefine what success means to you, beyond monetary wealth. On the following pages, you will find meditation journeys to help you reflect on your financial beliefs and practices.

**Meditation Journey Thirteen: Achieving Balance within the
Individual Pod**

Find a quiet place without distractions. Take a deep breath in. As
you exhale, release any tension from your body. Grant yourself
permission to take this time for yourself. Continue to breathe deeply.
With each inhale, draw in calmness. With each exhale, let go of any
stress. Feel yourself becoming more relaxed and centered.

Imagine you are visiting a futuristic place where you have an
individual pod designed for ultimate relaxation. The pod is uniquely
tailored to you, and you take a seat in the ergonomic chair, which
molds perfectly to your form. The ambient lighting adjusts to your
presence, starting with a calming pink hue that transitions to a

soothing blue. This special color encourages introspection. As you inhale the purified air, you sink further into the chair.

You see peaceful landscapes that represent your thoughts and feelings. Rolling hills covered in vibrant green grass transition into tranquil forests where sunlight filters through the trees. Birds chirp melodiously, their songs echoing while the soft rustle of leaves creates a soothing backdrop.

As the scene shifts, calm seas come into view, their rhythmic waves lapping onto a pristine shore. The sound of the waves mingles with the distant cries of seagulls, creating a serene coastal ambiance.

Feel the smooth, comfortable material of the chair cradling your body, offering support and security. The ambient lighting adjusts to a soothing glow, creating a cocoon of peace. With each breath, you synchronize with the tranquil scenes, feeling more connected to your inner calm.

Now, you think about your financial situation and the moments in your life when you had financial stability and weren't stressed. The pod's walls show scenes of you achieving milestones, whether buying a home, receiving a promotion, or simply enjoying worry-free time with loved ones. You see images of yourself purchasing the things you needed. Observe your life at that time and the surrounding people, your work, and your activities.

Think about your age, what you were doing, and what was occurring. Reflect on the feelings you had—perhaps security, joy, or gratitude. Maybe you thought it would always be like this and you felt secure. Allow yourself to re-experience these positive feelings and to see yourself during this time period.

Now you recall when there were rough patches in your financial journey. The pod's walls show challenging periods. Maybe you see yourself navigating a job loss, a dip in the market, a reduction in household income, or a significant expense you didn't see coming. Perhaps you were a student during this period or were at the beginning of your career. You see your life and the surrounding people at that time.

You recall what that was like for you. Recognize the emotions you experienced. How did you feel? Were you afraid, frustrated, angry, or upset? Now consider what this time in your life taught you. Did it make you more resilient? Did it shift your perspective on what's truly important in your life?

You realize that both the ups and downs of your financial life are integral parts of your journey. Each has contributed to your growth and understanding of what financial well-being means to you. They help you identify what is truly important. These memories make you who you are, and they have given you valuable wisdom.

Now you see a beautiful stream in the valley of a wide field surrounded by mountains. You realize this stream represents the fluid nature of your financial state. See yourself next to it, contemplating your current financial beliefs and attitudes, and gently consider that money is a resource, not a goal. And that sometimes resources, like this stream, can be plentiful and other times they can be scarce.

Consider the abundance in your life that goes beyond finances. Observe the images of the true wealth in your life that money can't buy. You see the valuable experiences you've had, the vacations, all the fun times, and the small joys that have enriched your life. Recall some happy memories with family and friends that have enriched your life.

Important people and wonderful relationships are a tremendous wealth. See the faces of loved ones who have supported and cared for you. See the people who are closest to you and who make your life what it is. Observe all the moments of connection, the shared laughter, the comforting hugs, and the words of encouragement.

You see the many people who have walked beside you on your journey: the friends who have celebrated your successes and stood by you during hard times. These relationships are the real treasures of your life, filling it with love, joy, and meaning.

Acknowledge the time spent outside of work as one of the greatest riches. You see the peaceful mornings, the leisurely afternoons, and the quiet evenings that have allowed you to rest and rejuvenate. These moments enable you to live fully, providing the free time to pursue your passions and nurture your well-being.

You watch the river flowing next to you. As you stand there, you see how it meanders through the landscape, adapting to the terrain it encounters, just as you navigate the highs and lows of your financial path. The river's steady flow, regardless of its volume, reminds you that your financial journey is also continuous and resilient. The sunlight dances on the surface of the water, symbolizing the many ways your life sparkles beyond money.

In this space, repeat this affirmation: "Abundance in my life is measured by the richness of my experiences and the depth of my relationships."

As you take a deep breath, let the sound of the flowing river wash over you, filling you with peace and assurance. Listen to the gentle gurgle of the water and reflect on how your life extends beyond material possessions, embracing the profound treasures of health, meaningful connections, and personal fulfillment.

When you're ready, gently return to your current environment, carrying a sense of clarity about your financial journey, empowered by realizations about true wealth.

Meditation Journey Fourteen: Crystal Cave

Begin by finding a quiet place where you can sit undisturbed. Take a deep breath in, and as you exhale slowly, release any stress in your muscles, any burdens weighing on your shoulders. Allow yourself to sink into the present moment, your body supported and your mind beginning to clear.

Imagine stepping away from the surface world and descending into an enchanted crystal cave. As you're transported down toward the cave, you feel lighter, leaving behind the weights of financial worries and desires for material wealth. The ambient sounds of the outside world fade away, replaced by a serene silence.

As you enter the cave, notice the gentle glow of the crystals illuminating the space with a soft, ethereal light. Each crystal radiates an energy that resonates with your own, welcoming you into this space. Within the cave, you are surrounded by a comforting stillness, interrupted only by the gentle, calming sound of a concealed subterranean stream. The walls of the cave shimmer with various hues—deep blues, calming greens, and soft purples. The air is cool and fresh, carrying a faint, earthy scent. As you walk deeper into the cave, the gentle light and atmosphere make you feel as though you have stepped into a world entirely devoted to your relaxation and well-being.

You approach a wall adorned with many crystals, each emitting a unique and calming energy. You notice a deep purple crystal, its surface smooth and inviting. Run your hands over it, feeling an immediate sense of relief as it seems to absorb any tension you're carrying. The crystal's warmth spreads through your fingertips, traveling up your arms and relaxing your entire body. You close your eyes for a moment, allowing the soothing energy to flow throughout your entire body.

Next, you notice a deep blue crystal projecting from the wall. Its surface is cool and smooth to the touch, evoking a sense of serenity. You then approach a deep green crystal. When you place your fingers across its jagged surface, it changes its hue to a light-green color.

Now, within this enchanted cave, you envision your life free from the constraints and pressures of financial obligations. You see an existence where these burdens dissolve into nothingness. You are no longer worried about money. Liberated from the chains of bills and the pursuit of material possessions, you find yourself truly free. What does this freedom look like? Is it a peaceful home free from clutter? Is it a schedule not dictated by payments and deadlines?

Visualize a life filled with simplicity and contentment. Your surroundings are minimalist yet rich with meaning, each item and moment carefully chosen to enhance your well-being. The environment is serene, perhaps with large windows that let in natural light, offering views of nature that soothe the soul. See the look of peace on your face as you no longer worry about money.

Let the crystals work their magic by filling you with these visions of a life free from financial worries. You see your daily life unfold in this new reality. You indulge in activities that awaken joy and fulfillment deep within you. Perhaps it's quality time with family and friends, exploring new things, or dedicating yourself to a passion. Maybe it's taking time to do something you always wanted to do, but that you have been putting off. Perhaps it's just relaxing and taking time for yourself. Who is there? What are you doing? What kind of life are you creating? See these scenes with clarity, noticing the details.

Perhaps you are spending mornings in a peaceful routine, enjoying a quiet cup of coffee or tea as the sun rises, bringing light into your day. During the day, you are engaged in work you have always wanted to do, or maybe you are taking it easy. Afternoons might be filled with meaningful activities—creative projects, leisurely walks in nature, or engaging in hobbies that bring you happiness. Evenings could be serene and restorative, spent in the company of loved ones, sharing stories, laughter, and a sense of belonging.

As you bask in the serenity of the crystal cave, reflect on what brings true richness to your life. Find the sources of genuine happiness and fulfillment that transcend money. See the important people in your life—family members and friends. Acknowledge that the essence of a meaningful life often rests in connections, experiences, and the journey of personal growth. Realize that these treasures are accessible to you, regardless of financial status. See what forms true abundance: love, joy, peace, and fulfillment—gems that no amount of money can buy.

Pay close attention to how you feel in this world without financial issues. Is there a sense of lightness? Do you breathe more freely? Let these feelings envelop you, providing you with tranquility and the profound sense of freedom. Notice how your body feels—relaxed, at ease, unencumbered by the stress of financial concerns. Your mind is clear, open to new possibilities, and filled with a sense of peace.

Contemplate how you can weave these insights into your current existence. Ask yourself how you might shift your focus towards activities and relationships that nurture your soul. Consider the steps you can take to cultivate a life rich in joy and purpose, even in the face of financial challenges.

Perhaps it's as simple as prioritizing time with loved ones, pursuing hobbies that bring you joy, or finding moments of stillness in your daily routine. Maybe it involves reevaluating your priorities, letting go of the desire for some material things, and finding contentment in the present moment. Each small step you take towards nurturing your well-being and fostering meaningful connections adds to the richness of your life.

Now, gently come back to your present environment. Carry with you the tranquility and clarity you've discovered in this crystal cave, a reminder of the inner peace and abundance available to you at any moment. Open your eyes and take a deep breath, feeling grounded and centered.

Chapter 5: Embracing Your Physical and Mental Health

Now I'd like to discuss something that touches every aspect of our lives—our health. This chapter encourages you to have compassion for yourself on your health journey, whether you are striving for certain goals, managing chronic conditions, or facing a health challenge.

Health is a complex aspect of our lives, influenced by genetics, environment, lifestyle, and even luck. It's crucial to recognize that our bodies are unique, and comparisons to others can often lead to feelings of inadequacy or self-blame. Each of us is on our own health journey in our own way.

Self-Blame and Compassion: It's easy to blame ourselves when facing health challenges or health goals and common to feel responsible for conditions beyond our control. However, self-compassion is a powerful antidote to self-blame.

Understanding Health as a Journey: Most health journeys are not linear, but rather a winding road with ups and downs. Setbacks and challenges are part of this journey, not indicators of personal failure. And along the way, you may feel many emotions. You may feel angry, sad, ashamed, fearful, or anxious. And you may feel sorry for yourself. That is normal. As you navigate these emotions, it's important to be compassionate.

Body Positivity and Self-Love: This chapter also touches on body positivity and self-love. It's essential to appreciate and care for your body, no matter its shape, size, or health status.

Above all, your current health does not define you. You are a complex, unique individual with dreams, aspirations, and inner strength. This chapter aims to empower you to be kind to yourself, no matter where you are on your journey. In the following section, you will find meditations to help you embrace your physical health. The subsequent section will focus on mental health.

Physical Health

Meditation Journey Fifteen: Mystical Spring

Find a comfortable place where you can sit or lie down, free from distractions. Take a deep breath in, allowing your lungs and belly to fill with air, and then exhale slowly, releasing any stress that you may be carrying. With each breath, let yourself sink deeper into relaxation. Take another deep breath, feeling your shoulders drop and your muscles loosen as you exhale. Let go of any thoughts or worries, focusing solely on this moment.

Imagine yourself transported to a tranquil, mystical spring nestled in a lush, green forest. The surroundings are vibrant, teeming with life and bathed in a light that glows with a soft, welcoming warmth. This spring is not just any body of water; it offers rejuvenation and the nurturing essence of nature. The air is filled with the sweet scent of blooming flowers and the earthy aroma of the forest floor. This beautiful spring has shimmering green waters that sparkle under the gentle sunlight. You feel you're being invited to come closer and partake in its healing properties.

As you approach the edge of the spring, you notice a profound sense of peace washing over you. The worries and stresses of everyday life seem to fade away, replaced by a deep calm. The air around the spring feels almost magical. You feel you are meant to be here at this moment and that this water is exactly what you need right now.

You dip your toes into the warm waters of the spring, and immediately a soothing sensation spreads through your body. The water washes away any tension and you relax. As you stand at the water's edge, take a moment to reflect on your body from head to toe. Do so without judgment, simply noting any areas of tension, discomfort, or pain. Acknowledge these feelings with compassion, understanding that they are a part of your experience.

Gradually, you walk deeper into the spring, feeling the warm water rising around your legs, surrounding them with a warming sensation. As you immerse yourself, the water reaches up to your middle, and eventually your neck, offering comfort. The buoyancy of the water allows your muscles to loosen, relieving pressure on your joints. Each gentle movement in the water feels effortless, as the healing properties of the spring surround you, soothing aches and revitalizing tired limbs. This warm water completely envelops you, making you feel weightless and at ease.

As you float, you notice a light emanating from deep within the water. This light rises and encircles your body, wrapping you in a gentle glow. This light represents self-compassion, an essential component of healing and personal growth. With each minute, this vibrant light fills you with warmth and kindness. It encourages you to release any harsh judgments you may hold against yourself, reminding you that you are on a unique journey, doing the best you can.

Take a moment to acknowledge the efforts you've made and the challenges you've faced. Recognize that self-compassion isn't just about feeling better in the moment—it's about building a foundation of kindness and understanding that supports you every day. Appreciate all that your body has done for you, the strength it has shown, and the resilience it has demonstrated. Understand that healing is a process, one that requires patience and self-love.

Now, take a deep breath and allow yourself to submerge beneath the surface of the water. Feel the healing energy from this magical spring permeating every cell of your body, cleansing and renewing you. As you come up for air, reflect on any current health challenges and extend words of encouragement to yourself. Silently affirm:

"I am on my unique health journey, and I am doing my best."

"My body deserves love and kindness, especially from myself."

"Healing has ups and downs, and I can navigate these with understanding and compassion."

As you continue to immerse yourself in the healing waters, visualize yourself taking positive steps towards your health goals. See yourself making choices that honor and respect your body, nurturing it with love and care. Whisper to yourself, "I am taking steps towards well-being." Envision yourself establishing daily routines that enhance your well-being, balancing activity with rest, and listening attentively to your body's needs. Remember that every small action counts, and that progress begins with small steps. You do not need to be perfect.

The magical, warm waters continue to surround and comfort you. As you immerse yourself in this sensation, your mind fills with compassionate thoughts, while the rejuvenating powers of the spring work their wonders. You float in this state of bliss, appreciating how far you've come on your personal journey. Allow yourself to accept where you are right now, with all your strengths and vulnerabilities.

Now it's time to leave the mystical spring. When you feel ready, float over to the edge of the spring. Step out of the water, feeling refreshed, hopeful, and filled with an appreciation for your body.

Meditation Journey Sixteen: Ethereal Energy Spa

Find a quiet and comfortable place where you can relax without any interruptions. Begin by taking a few deep, calming breaths. Inhale deeply, filling your lungs completely with air, and then exhale slowly. With each breath, feel your body relax more deeply, letting go of the day's worries and allowing your mind to become calm and focused.

Imagine you're visiting the Ethereal Energy Spa, a serene sanctuary that exists in a parallel realm of healing and rejuvenation. This spa is unlike any other; it floats amidst the cosmos, surrounded by stars, galaxies, and vibrant nebulae. The Ethereal Energy Spa harnesses the purest energies of the universe, offering a space where every moment brings you closer to profound healing and inner calm. Here, time feels different—slower, more tranquil—as if the usual rules of the physical world gently give way to the timeless power of energy.

As you enter the spa, you become aware of an almost imperceptible cosmic energy in the air. This subtle sound resonates with the deepest parts of your being, making you feel at ease. The building itself is a masterpiece, constructed from materials that seem both ancient and futuristic. Walls shimmer with an ethereal blue and purple light, softly pulsating as if alive with the energy they contain. The floors beneath your feet appear to float, giving you the sensation of weightlessness and freedom.

You go down a long, softly lit hallway, each step bringing you deeper into this haven of healing. You feel drawn to a particular room—a healing chamber that is filled with a soothing, warm light, promising restoration. As you enter, the calming glow of candles accentuates the peaceful atmosphere, casting gentle shadows that dance along the walls. You lie down on a unique bed made of soft, glowing energy, which contours completely to your body. This bed adjusts to your shape, providing unparalleled support and comfort as you sink deeper into relaxation.

As you rest on this energy bed, take a moment to reflect on your current health. You may notice a range of emotions—anger, sadness, frustration, fear, or even self-pity. Acknowledge these feelings without judgment; they are natural responses to the challenges you may be facing. Allow yourself to sit with these emotions, understanding that they are part of your journey. Recognize that this is a safe space to process your feelings and that it's okay to feel vulnerable here.

Now, the healing energies of the spa start to work their wonders. A cascade of healing light descends from above, bathing you in radiant brilliance. You feel this subtle energy energize and relax you at the same time. The light, infused with the essence of stars and the purity of the cosmos, penetrates every cell of your body. It moves gently yet powerfully, targeting areas of discomfort, tension, or disease, infusing them with healing energy. You feel this cosmic force unravel any knots of pain or stress, dissolving them into shadows that fade away into the light.

Lying there, you reflect on the remarkable journey your body has taken with you. It has carried you through life's many experiences, both joyful and challenging. You feel grateful for all it has done, acknowledging even the moments when it may not have met your expectations. Extend compassion to your body for enduring stress, illness, and any harsh judgments you have placed upon it. Appreciate the incredible creation that is your body, which has been with you since the beginning, constantly working to support you.

Reflecting on your life's journey, you realize that the path to health and well-being is rarely straightforward. It is filled with both mountains and valleys, with achievements and setbacks. Each step forward, no matter how small, contributes to your overall well-being. Understand that setbacks are natural and are opportunities to learn and adapt, not signs of failure. They are part of the journey, helping you to grow stronger and wiser.

As the healing energy flows through you, recognize the inherent strength and healing capacity of your body. With each breath, this energy sinks deeper, rejuvenating you. See your health challenges gradually dissolving, replaced by a newfound vibrancy and strength. Picture yourself achieving your wellness goals, whether it's recovering from an illness, reaching a personal milestone, or attaining complete physical and emotional well-being. This energy envelops you, permeating every cell, easing tension, and clearing your mind, making room for healing thoughts and self-acceptance.

With every breath, allow this soothing energy to work its magic, bolstering your body's natural resilience. As you bask in this peaceful state, a profound calm anchors you, affirming your body's ability to heal.

Now, turn your focus inward to the core of your being, where a spark of this same cosmic energy resides. Feel this inner light growing stronger, fueled by the healing energies of the spa. Recognize that this power—the ability to heal and rejuvenate—is always within you, waiting to be tapped into. As you breathe deeply, repeat affirmations that resonate with this truth:

"I am whole and healing."

"I am infused with the healing energy of the universe."

"I trust in my body's ability to heal itself."

"I am grateful for the healing that is occurring in my body right now."

Spend as much time as you want in the Ethereal Energy Spa, soaking in the healing energies. Allow yourself to fully absorb this experience, knowing that the benefits will continue to unfold even after you leave this space.

Now, it's time to leave the spa. It's available to you any time you need to visit. When you feel ready, come back to your current environment, carrying the healing energy into your day or evening.

Mental Health

Now I'd like to discuss a crucial yet often overlooked aspect of our lives: our mental health. In a society that frequently emphasizes physical health and tangible accomplishments, the importance of mental well-being can sometimes be overshadowed. However, acknowledging and nurturing our mental health is essential.

Mental health encompasses our emotional, psychological, and social well-being. It influences how we think, feel, and act. Good mental health helps us to lead fulfilling lives, form healthy relationships, and adapt to change. Embracing mental health allows us to develop resilience to navigate life's challenges and recover from setbacks. Understanding and working through mental health issues can lead to significant personal growth.

In this section, I offer meditation journeys to help you cultivate a healthy mental state, cope with the stresses of daily life, and develop a deeper understanding of your emotional landscape.

It's important to note that seeking professional help is a sign of strength, not weakness. Embracing mental health is a journey towards a more balanced, fulfilled, and compassionate life.

Meditation Journey Seventeen: Magical Treehouse

Find a comfortable, quiet place where you can unwind without interruptions. Begin by taking deep, calming breaths. With each inhale, draw in a feeling of peacefulness. With each exhale, release any tension or worries. Let your body relax completely, feeling lighter with each breath. Allow your mind to ease, letting go of any worries.

Imagine a secure, cozy treehouse nestled in the heart of a tropical rainforest. This treehouse rests high among the branches of a sturdy, ancient tree. It serves as an elevated retreat from the world, offering safety, comfort, and a panoramic view of the rainforest. The tree's deep roots and the surrounding lush greenery represent stability, growth, and the interconnectedness of life.

You stand at the base of this ancient tree. Wooden stairs provide a way up to this wondrous treehouse. You grasp the smooth wooden railing and ascend the stairs on the side of the tree step by step. When you enter the treehouse, you notice how the space is bathed in a warm, golden light, creating a serene atmosphere. The air here is fresh and filled with sounds of the rainforest—birdsong and the whisper of gentle breezes.

The treehouse is large, far exceeding your expectations. It features several rooms and even boasts a second floor. Each room is furnished with plush furniture and soft cushions, creating inviting nooks designed for relaxation and a retreat from the stresses of daily life. As you explore, you discover a cozy room. Here, you settle into a pile of soft, plush cushions that mold perfectly to your form, providing comfort and support. With each breath, you feel yourself sinking deeper into a state of relaxation, completely embraced by the safe environment of the treehouse.

You now think about your mental well-being and any current struggles you're having. Perhaps you're feeling hopeless, unmotivated, sad, angry, depressed, or maybe you're just not feeling good about yourself. It's important to realize that many of these feelings will pass. And many things that we struggle with get better over time. As you feel secure in the treehouse, say these words of encouragement to yourself.

"Just as the rainforest embraces change, I accept my emotions as a natural part of life."

"I am worthy of compassion and care, just like the trees are worthy of sun and rain."

"I deserve to feel good about myself because I am worthy."

"My current struggles don't define me."

Take a moment to enjoy the secure space, open and airy, illuminated by the soft, comforting light that surrounds you. Acknowledge any thoughts or emotions that surface, visualizing them as leaves that grow, change color, and then drift to the ground. Realize that our emotions come and go like the leaves, falling away naturally, leaving the tree—your core—steady and unshaken. Embrace the cycle of renewal. Even the leaves that fall nourish the soil, contributing to new growth.

You now think about the things in your life that bring you joy and contentment. It could be the love of family and friends, personal achievements, or simple pleasures. Consider all the things that you love and recall some happy memories from your life.

Remind yourself that it's okay to have difficult days. It's okay to feel overwhelmed or anxious at times. These experiences are part of being human. Offer yourself understanding. Acknowledge that life can be hard, you are not perfect, and emotional challenges are common.

As you continue to breathe deeply, imagine the tree's roots, strong and widespread, anchoring deep into the earth. These roots are like your own foundations—your values, experiences, and relationships—that provide stability and nourishment. Just as the tree draws sustenance from its roots to flourish, remind yourself that you also can draw on your resources to foster resilience and growth.

As you rise from your seat, a gentle rainfall starts in the rainforest, drawing your attention as you glance out the window. The raindrops lightly tap on the leaves and roof of the treehouse. This rain symbolizes the challenges we sometimes face. However, just as the rain brings essential water that revitalizes, your challenges can also lead to growth and renewal.

As the rain eases, a beautiful rainbow arcs across the sky, a reminder of hope and renewal following adversity. Allow the colors of the rainbow to enhance your feelings of peace and optimism. You admire this bright rainbow out of the treehouse window. Each color offers you something important.

Red gives you strength and vitality,

Orange gives you creativity and enthusiasm,
Yellow gives you joy and optimism,
Green gives you harmony and balance,
Blue gives you calm and healing,
Violet gives you intuition and perception,
White gives you spiritual fulfillment and inner peace.

The colors are intense. The rainbow grows brighter and illuminates the entire forest. You reach out for the color that speaks to you most. When you touch that color, you experience the gift that color provides. Take a moment to absorb it.

Feeling better, you go back to the stairs of the treehouse and make your way down. As you reach the base of the tree, look back at the treehouse, knowing that you can return to this safe, nurturing space at any time you need.

Like the tree, you are resilient, rooted deeply, and capable of weathering any storm. Like the forest, you are part of a larger ecosystem, connected to the world in meaningful ways, and capable of renewal and growth. Now come back to your present environment and take these feelings into your day or evening.

Meditation Journey Eighteen: Floating Sky Island

Begin by finding a comfortable spot where you can relax without interruptions. Take a deep breath in, filling your lungs as fully as you can. As you exhale, imagine yourself gently lifting off the ground, rising up into the sky. With each breath, you ascend higher, leaving behind the familiar landscapes of your daily life. You rise through layers of clouds and mist, feeling weightless as you float upward.

As you continue to ascend, you approach a breathtaking floating island, suspended effortlessly among the clouds—a place of serenity. Here, the usual worries and constraints of the world dissolve, replaced by a sense of freedom. As you draw closer, you see lush, vibrant gardens, gentle streams, and a landscape painted in rich greens and blues, symbolizing the healing power of nature and the vastness of possibilities.

The island's breathtaking beauty amazes you as you glide closer. The landscape is filled with sapphire rivers and towering trees covered in emerald leaves, as well as tall flowers everywhere. You land gently, feeling the soft grass beneath your feet. The air here is extraordinarily pure. You take a deep breath, filling your lungs with the crisp, clean air. The soothing sounds of a gurgling stream make you feel as if you've landed in another world.

As you explore this sanctuary, you are struck by the carnations and daffodils, which are extraordinarily large but have graceful petals. Many blooms tower above you, their oversized petals displaying an array of intense colors, ranging from deep, velvety purples to brilliant, fiery oranges and pastel pinks. These magnificent flowers grow in clusters that seem to reach for the sky. Their sheer size is a testament to this nurturing environment.

These flowers fill the air with their heady scent, delicate fragrance, and sweet perfume. These scents blend harmoniously, creating an intoxicating bouquet that dances on the breeze, with each fragrance briefly touching you before gently fading away. The combination of the lush, towering flora and the rich tapestry of aromas makes this place feel like a paradise.

As you walk around, you feel the lush grass underfoot and the soft petals brushing against you. You find a quiet spot near a small, crystal-clear stream and sit on a soft patch of grass. Breathing in the pure air, you feel a sense of lightness envelop you.

In this moment, you allow your mind to wander to your emotional struggles. Perhaps you've been grappling with feelings of inadequacy, anxiety, or frustration. Maybe you've felt sadness, anger, or simply a sense of dissatisfaction with yourself. It's possible that you've been experiencing a loss of energy and hope. As you sit in this beautiful place, it's important to acknowledge these feelings, not as flaws or weaknesses, but as natural parts of the human experience that everyone encounters.

As breathe deeply, soften any negative self-judgments you may hold. Remind yourself: "I am not alone. Many people experience these difficulties." With each breath, focus on sending compassion inward, filling you with kindness and understanding. Let these thoughts come to mind:

"I've faced emotional struggles before; they are part of life."

"I am doing my best with the resources I have."

"I am on a journey, and this is part of it."

These affirmations are not just words; they are truths that resonate with your deepest self. They acknowledge your journey, your struggles, and the resilience you demonstrate daily.

As you look into the stream beside you, you observe the stones within it. Some stones lie still, while others tumble and shift with the current. Reach into the cool stream and select a stone. Feel its wet surface, texture, and weight; notice its imperfections. This stone is a symbol of your own journey—unique, shaped by the surrounding forces.

As you hold the stone in your hand, let it remind you of your strength and resilience and self-compassion you have cultivated. Feel its shape and weight, grounding you in the knowledge that you carry this strength into your daily life. The stone, like you, is unique and has its own journey, marked by ups and downs. Acknowledge that you have been shaped by various life experiences, yet you continue to persevere. And being human means experiencing a range of emotions along your journey. Repeat these affirmations to yourself:

"I embrace my feelings as guides, not enemies."

"Each day, I grow stronger and more capable of managing life's difficulties."

"I choose to speak to myself with love and encouragement."

Like this stone, you are a strong entity in the river of life. Allow these affirmations to become a part of your inner dialogue. As you sit surrounded by the beauty of the floating island, let this moment of peace and self-compassion solidify within you.

As you prepare to leave this serene sanctuary, take the stone you selected as a token of your visit. The stone in your hand symbolizes your journey through life's turbulent streams, a reminder of your resilience and strength. Like the stone, you may be pushed and pulled by the currents of life, but you remain strong and enduring, shaped yet unbroken by your experiences.

With this feeling of peacefulness and resolve, you gently lift off the island, floating back towards your earthly realm. This place of serenity is always within your mind, a sanctuary you can return to whenever you need it.

You slowly descend through the clouds. As you are gently lowered back into your current world, carry these feelings and thoughts int your day or evening.

Chapter 6: Embracing Past Mistakes

There is certainly one universal aspect of our human experience: our past mistakes. No matter who we are, we have all made choices that we regret. These past mistakes can loom large in our minds, affecting our self-esteem and influencing our present lives.

Mistakes are an inevitable part of being human. They range from minor blunders to significant misjudgments, and their impact can vary. However, it's not uncommon for us to hold on to these errors, allowing them to color our view of ourselves and our capabilities.

The problem with dwelling on past mistakes is that it keeps us tethered to moments we cannot change, trapping us in a cycle of guilt and regret. This not only hinders our ability to enjoy the present but also affects our perception of the future. It can lead to a fear of taking risks or trying new things, because we worry about making more mistakes.

The key to dealing with past mistakes is not to dwell on them, but to learn from them and forgive oneself. This is easier said than done, but it's a crucial step. Every mistake has the potential to teach us something valuable. Whether it's about our values, our decision-making process, or our interactions with others, there is always a lesson to be learned. And forgiving ourselves allows us to acknowledge our mistakes without letting them define us. By releasing the hold of our past mistakes, we free ourselves to fully engage with the present and embrace new opportunities. And accepting and moving past mistakes makes us more resilient. It teaches us we can endure setbacks and grow stronger from them.

The meditation journeys in this chapter will help you come to terms with your past mistakes. My goal is to guide you towards a place of self-forgiveness and acceptance. You'll learn to view your past not as a series of missteps, but as a valuable part of your life's journey.

Embracing your past mistakes is not about forgetting them or excusing them. It's about understanding their role in shaping who you are today and using that knowledge to move forward with compassion and confidence.

Meditation Journey Nineteen: Letting Go at Rock Lake

Find a quiet and comfortable place to sit. This is your time for introspection and self-care. As you settle into this quiet place, take a deep, calming breath. Inhale slowly, drawing in feelings of peacefulness. Exhale gently, releasing any tension or stress from your body. Do this repeatedly, taking in several deep, calming breaths. Allow yourself to fully relax and be present in this moment.

Imagine you are at a tranquil lake with a rocky shore. You see rocks of various sizes scattered along the shoreline in front of you. They vary in color—some are dark gray, others are lighter gray, and a few are almost white. Many are covered in algae beneath the water, suggesting they have been there for a long time. Others lie outside the water, basking in the sunlight. Each rock represents a mistake someone has made. Some lie on the shore, some rest just below the surface, and many are at the bottom of this lake of compassion.

Think about a past mistake you've made—it might be a significant regret or a minor one. Recall the times you often revisit this memory with self-criticism. Instead of harsh judgment, approach these memories with an open, understanding heart.

As these recollections surface, acknowledge the emotions they bring. You might encounter feelings of guilt, shame, sadness, or disappointment. Allow yourself to experience these emotions, recognizing them as a normal response to making mistakes and being human.

Consider this past mistake and what led to it. Take a moment to reflect on the specific circumstances and challenges you were facing at that time. Were there any personal or professional issues that weighed heavily on you? Perhaps you were experiencing stress from work, family responsibilities, or other commitments that made life difficult. It's also possible that you were dealing with emotional or psychological pressures, such as anxiety, depression, or a sense of being overwhelmed. These factors can cloud judgment and affect how we handle situations. Additionally, think about the resources you had at your disposal. Were you lacking time, financial stability, or support from others? Sometimes, having limited resources can force us to make decisions out of necessity rather than choice, and these decisions might not always align with our long-term goals or values.

Consider the information you had at the time. Often mistakes happen because we are working with incomplete or incorrect information. Maybe you were not fully aware of all the options available to you, or perhaps you didn't know or misunderstood certain facts. In the heat of the moment, you likely made the best decision you could with the knowledge you had. It's important to acknowledge that our understanding is always evolving, and hindsight often provides clarity that wasn't accessible in the moment. This recognition can help you see the situation more objectively and understand that a lack of complete information influenced your actions.

It's crucial to recognize that, like everyone, you were striving for happiness and doing your best at that time. You were a different person back then, shaped by different experiences, knowledge, and perspectives. This self-reflection is not about self-criticism, but rather understanding and compassion. By acknowledging your growth and the lessons learned, you can see this mistake as part of your personal development rather than a defining failure. Remember, everyone makes mistakes; it's a universal part of the human experience. Many others have made the same mistake that you did.

As you look along the shore, find the rock that represents your mistake. Even if you think it will be too heavy to pick up, approach the rock and try. Notice its color, the ridges on it, and any cracks. Place your hands on the rock and then try to pick it up. Surprisingly, it's light enough for you to lift, regardless of its size. Feel its texture, its weight, and its density. This rock represents a burden you've been carrying, a tangible symbol of this mistake that has added weight to your life's journey.

You lift the rock, and as you hold it, you reflect on its significance. It has a purpose; it's not just a burden, but also a teacher. You reflect on the lessons this mistake has taught you. Maybe it taught you the significance of patience, honesty, or hard work. Perhaps it's taught you about a person or a situation. Maybe it has taught you a painful lesson about acting hastily or letting emotions guide your choices. Whatever the lesson is, think about the growth and understanding it has brought into your life. This rock, this mistake, has pushed you towards greater self-awareness. You acknowledge what you have learned and how it has shaped and strengthened you. You are wiser now as a result, even if this is a painful recollection.

Now, with a heart full of gratitude, you thank this mistake for the wisdom it has provided. You realize mistakes are an important part of everyone's life. They are the rough edges that refine us, the challenges that strengthen us and make us wiser. Mistakes are inevitable, and we all make them. As you hold this rock, take a moment to be thankful for the lessons it has brought, for the person it has helped you become.

You approach the lake, feeling the rough texture of the rock against your skin and its weight in your hands. As you reach the water's edge, you throw the rock into the lake with all your strength.

It sails through the air, cutting through the stillness, and for a moment, time seems to pause. Then, with a satisfying "plunk," it hits the water, sending droplets flying. You hear the distinct sound of it breaking the surface, followed by the gentle rhythm of ripples forming.

You watch as the ripples expand outward in perfect circles, the once-smooth surface of the lake now alive with movement. The circles grow larger, spreading outward. You feel a sense of release, knowing that the weight of your mistake is now at the bottom of the lake.

The ripples extend out to the shore, gradually fading until the lake returns to its state of calm. The rock, your mistake, now rests at the bottom of the lake, out of sight but not forgotten. It has served its purpose, and now you can move forward, feeling lighter and freer, with the lesson it has given you. As you admire this azure lake, you say these affirmations to yourself:

"I forgive myself for my past mistake."

"I release the past and embrace the present with an open heart."

"I am more than my mistake; I am on a journey of growth."

Let these statements sink in and forgive yourself. Now, you walk away from the lake, leaving your mistake behind. You move down a bright forest path feeling confident, self-assured, and unburdened. You have a lightness in your step, a smile on your face, and you're ready to face new challenges and embrace opportunities.

Now come back to your current environment. Carry this feeling with you into your day or evening.

Meditation Journey Twenty: Mystical Time Chamber

Find a quiet space where you can be comfortable and relaxed. Allow yourself to settle into this moment. Begin by taking several deep, slow breaths. Feel the air filling your lungs and then release it slowly, letting go of any tightness in your body. Repeat this several times, taking lengthy, deep breaths.

Imagine a mystical time chamber, a place where you can go back in time. This chamber, a small room made with an eclectic mixture of ancient wood and metals, serves as a gateway, allowing for a compassionate journey back to when you made a mistake.

As you enter this chamber, you see dials and knobs protruding from a machine engulfed in golden light. Old books from long ago line the many shelves on either side of the machine. A soft glow fills the room, and the gentle hum of the machine permeates the air. You have the feeling that anything is possible as you stand in this place. You breathe in and exhale slowly, ready to embark on a journey into the past.

Approach the machine and touch the large, smooth golden knob in the middle of it. Almost immediately, the chamber's energy activates, creating a gentle vibration under your feet. The chamber door shuts and the walls shimmer, signaling the start of your temporal journey. As the energy amplifies, a portal opens, revealing a moment in your past where you made a significant mistake. Step forward into that time period to observe it with an intention to understand and offer compassion, not criticism. No one can see you in this time period, but you can see everyone clearly, including yourself.

You are now back in that moment in time, right before making a mistake. You see the other people who are present. What was happening right before this moment? Consider your life and all the things that were happening then. What was your work situation? How was your family life? What major events were occurring then?

You consider the emotional state of your past self in that time period right before making this mistake. What were you feeling? Recall the struggles you were experiencing. Acknowledge that emotional states influence decisions and actions. Your past self may have been trying to navigate complex emotions and feelings.

You think about the circumstances that led to this mistake. Consider the knowledge and experience you had back then. What did you believe and how did this influence your behavior? How did you navigate the situation? How did you cope with stress? Understand that your past self was working with a different understanding than you have now.

You ponder the resources that were available to you. Resources aren't just financial or material. They include support systems, like family and friends, and internal resources, like resilience and coping mechanisms. Did you have access to good support? How did the people around you help or hinder you?

As you reflect on these various aspects of your life, you feel compassion for your past self, who is about to make this mistake. See yourself clearly in this moment and recognize that you were doing the best you could with the knowledge, emotional maturity, and resources you had at the time. Your actions weren't driven by malice or incompetence, but were instead a result of limited perspective and capability. This realization allows you to forgive your past self, acknowledging that you were doing what you thought was best at that moment. Remember that you didn't have the benefit of hindsight or the wisdom you've gained since then. You were navigating your path as best as you knew how.

Now, you watch the mistake occur. Notice the sequence of events and your reactions. See how your past self tried to handle the situation with the tools and understanding available. Observe without judgment as the mistake unfolds.

Now, offer compassion to your past self. Send them a silent message. "I understand why you made this choice. You were doing your best under difficult circumstances. I forgive you for this mistake. It was a learning experience for you."

You understand this mistake has been part of your growth. Acknowledge the lessons it has taught you and how it has shaped your journey. Consider the strength, understanding, or resilience that has come from this experience.

From a place of empathy and understanding, extend compassion to your past self. Envision a warm, comforting light emerging from your heart, symbolizing forgiveness and acceptance. Watch as this light reaches out to your past self, touching them and surrounding them.

You see your past self relaxing with this forgiveness, their burdens easing as they absorb your compassion. Your past self now understands that they are not defined by this moment, but are a part of a larger, evolving journey. As your past self continues to bask in this warm, comforting light, they feel a sense of peace. They seem to understand that this light is a gift from you—a gesture of unconditional love and understanding from the person they will become. They now know there is a bright future awaiting them. Imagine them smiling, a genuine smile that reflects a newfound inner peace and acceptance.

Now come back to the time chamber, bringing this compassion for your past self. Know that this Mystical Time Chamber is always available to you. A place where you can heal and reconcile with your past. When you feel ready, return to your present environment, bringing this feeling into your day or evening.

Meditation Journey Twenty-One: The Enchanted Mansion

Find a quiet and comfortable place where you will not be disturbed. Take a few moments to settle into a relaxed position. Begin by taking deep, cleansing breaths. Inhale slowly, and as you exhale, feel more and more relaxed. Take several additional deep breaths. Let any worries dissolve away and allow your body to slip into a state of calmness.

Imagine an enchanted mansion that has leaped straight from the pages of a fantasy novel yet has an undeniable realism. The mansion stands grandly with an imposing gray stone exterior, its weathered façade radiating both strength and timeless beauty. Tall turrets crowned with conical slate roofs rise gracefully, giving the structure a fairytale appearance. Curved windows crafted with leaded glass peek out from the walls, reflecting the sun. Ivy and wisteria intertwine around the stone base, softening the mansion's formidable presence with cascades of green and bursts of purple blooms.

Balconies and verandas, adorned with wrought-iron railings, jut out at various levels, offering places to sit and relax. Stone gargoyles perch on the corners of the roof, their watchful eyes taking in the surrounding vista. As you approach the mansion, you see a magnificent set of marble steps. The enormous front doors, intricately carved from wood, complemented by a large circular stained-glass window that emits a comforting glow, making this building captivating.

You feel drawn to this mansion, pulled by the allure of its appearance and the feeling that something magical will happen here. And you're right. This is a mansion where each room helps visitors confront and heal from their past. A magical place crafted for transformation.

As you stand at the grand entrance of the mansion, the doors open before you with a gentle, inviting creak and you feel welcomed inside. You step into the entryway, finding yourself in front of a large wooden staircase adorned with a rich purple carpet that ascends to the second floor. You walk up the stairs, and before you is a vast hallway lined with doors of all different hues. Each door is unique, representing different parts of the human experience, from joy and sorrow to love and regret. But today, a purple door calls to you more loudly than the others—the Door of Forgiveness.

With a deep, calming breath, you approach this door, your hand resting on the knob, feeling a warm, pulsating energy. As you gently push it open, you step into a room bathed in soft, golden light, filled with comfortable deep purple furnishings that invite you to relax and let go.

You sink into a plum-colored armchair in front of an ornate mirror that resembles a work of art. The mirror stands tall, enclosed within a deep purple frame adorned with scrolls and floral motifs that weave around its perimeter.

The glass of the mirror looks mysteriously fogged over. It obscures the reflection slightly, lending a mystical quality to it as if it is not merely a mirror, but a gateway to another dimension. As you relax in the armchair, the room's tranquil atmosphere surrounds you and prepares you for a healing journey.

Gradually, the mirror becomes less foggy, and images appear. At first, they are blurry and indistinct, but as they sharpen, a scene of your past mistake comes into view. Although you want to look away, the enchanted mansion enables you to confront this image with understanding. The mirror vividly displays this mistake, playing out the scene within its dark violet frame. You see yourself, the error you made, and all the contributing factors—the thoughts and feelings you harbored and all the things that were happening in your life at that time.

As you watch this mistake, a gentle voice reassures you that you are human, and that everyone makes mistakes. This voice is reassuring, and wise. It explains that you need to forgive yourself, emphasizing that mistakes are inevitable parts of our journey, shaping who we are. The voice tells you that you need to be kind to yourself. As you listen, you feel empathy towards your past self within the safety of the enchanted mansion.

Now the mirror shows you the people affected by your actions. You see them clearly, experiencing their pain. As the impact of your actions unfolds before you, the gentle voice reassures you, "It's important to see and understand the pain you have caused, not as a punishment, but as a step towards healing."

This voice encourages you to extend feelings of compassion toward each person affected by this mistake. As you see each of them, a purple light radiates from you toward the mirror. Imbued with love and compassion, this gentle light flows from you, surrounding the individuals you've affected. The voice continues, "By sending this light, you are actively taking part in the healing of both yourself and those you've hurt. This is a powerful act of compassion."

You see this healing light soothing their emotional wounds, bringing them a sense of peace. As this light surrounds them, it lifts their feelings of pain and makes them receptive to seeing you without a deep sense of hurt.

Now, the gentle voice guides you, explaining how you can communicate through the mirror and ask for their forgiveness. "Tell them you sincerely regret any pain you caused and that your intention is to foster healing and understanding."

You look into the mirror, your gaze steady, and with a deep sense of sincerity, you tell them how much you regret your actions and how deeply you wish for their forgiveness. You assure them you did not intend to hurt them, but you acknowledge the significant effect that your actions had on them. Say whatever you need to tell them.

As you watch, they respond to your request for forgiveness. They see the sincerity and depth of your remorse. They respond with an open heart, acknowledging your apology, and offering you their forgiveness. See the moment they release negative feelings towards you, a symbolic gesture of letting go and moving on. They no longer carry a burden. Witness their expressions softening, signaling a release of any resentment they may have held onto. You see them in the mirror feeling contented.

The mirror now shows you an image of them continuing with their lives, no longer burdened by the past incident. They find happiness and fulfillment, their smiles genuine and their hearts light. Feel the joy in knowing that they are free from the hurt and are living their lives to the fullest.

You feel a sense of closure. The mirror returns to its original foggy appearance, just as it was when you first sat down. You take a deep breath. When you're ready, stand up from the armchair, carrying with you the peace and compassion you've discovered here. As you close the Door of Forgiveness softly behind you, know that the enchanted mansion is always available for whenever you need its magic.

Come back to your present environment, carrying these feelings with you into your day or evening.

Chapter 7: Embracing Life Transitions

Life is a constant journey of change and transformation. From the moment we are born, we are in a state of perpetual motion, evolving, adapting, and navigating our life's journey. There are so many transitions—pivotal moments when we move from one phase of life to another.

Transitions are an intrinsic part of the human experience. They can take many forms, from the milestones of childhood to the unexpected twists and turns of adulthood. Whether we're embarking on a new career path, entering parenthood, or facing the loss of a loved one, transitions are unavoidable.

Although transitions are a natural and essential part of life, they are not always easy. Sometimes, when we find ourselves in the midst of change, we blame ourselves. We may criticize ourselves for the transition, believing we should have been better prepared or made different choices. We may also blame ourselves for the emotional turmoil that goes along with change, thinking we should handle it with more grace and ease.

I want to encourage you to view life transitions through a lens of self-compassion. Transitions should be embraced as a fundamental aspect of our existence. Each transition, no matter how challenging, offers us an opportunity for growth, self-discovery, and resilience.

In this chapter, the meditation journeys will help you view major life transitions with more compassion. Transitions are undoubtedly hard. However, we can make them more difficult if we are harsh on ourselves during significant life changes. And that can have ripple effects on others. It can cause us to act severely towards those we love, when we most need their support. Self-compassion reminds us it's not about avoiding the discomfort of transitions, but acknowledging our human vulnerability and treating ourselves with kindness and understanding.

Meditation Journey Twenty-Two: Bridge of Transitions

Find a quiet and comfortable place where you can take time for yourself. Begin by taking a few deep, cleansing breaths. Inhale deeply through your nose, feeling your chest and abdomen rise as you fill your lungs with air. Hold your breath for a moment, then exhale slowly. Repeat this process several times, each breath bringing you a deeper state of calmness. As you breathe, feel your shoulders drop, and let your body become heavy with relaxation. Fully immerse yourself in this moment.

Now, imagine standing at the start of a bridge made of sturdy wood and solid metal handrails spanning a gently flowing river. It stretches out before you, inviting you to cross. The air is cool, carrying the scent of the river and the surrounding plants on the banks. You take a deep breath, drawing in this fresh air, and wonder how many people have crossed this bridge. The sound of water moving beneath the bridge serves as a gentle reminder of life's constant flow and the transitions we all must navigate. This setting is a perfect place for reflection.

As you stand at the beginning of this bridge, think about the life transition you are currently facing or one that you expect will happen soon. It could be a new job, a change in relationship status, a move to a new place, or any significant shift in your life. This bridge represents this transition with a clear path in front of you. It is structurally sound, stretching from one side of the river to the other. It is safe.

Before you cross, take a moment to acknowledge the emotions this transition evokes. Allow yourself to feel them without judgment—whether it's excitement, fear, uncertainty, or a mix of different emotions. These feelings are natural responses to change. As you breathe deeply, imagine the river below, its gentle flow reassuring you that change is a natural part of life, something to be embraced rather than feared. The river's constant movement mirrors the inevitable transitions we all experience.

As you prepare to step onto the bridge, let self-kindness fill you, reminding you to be kind to yourself during challenging times. Transitions can be difficult, and it's important to treat yourself with understanding. As you get ready to cross the bridge, say these affirmations to yourself:

"I can navigate this change with grace and strength."

"I embrace this transition with an open heart."

"I allow myself to move forward with confidence and courage."

Take a moment to focus on any self-criticism you might have regarding this transition. We often judge ourselves harshly for the challenges we face, sometimes even for the need to make a transition at all. Remember, changes are an inevitable part of life, and struggling with them does not define your worth or capability—it simply reminds you of your humanity. The sounds of the river below remind you that all things change and flow onward.

Feel the solid support of the bridge beneath your feet and the handrails with their solid grip. Each step forward is a testament to your ability to face change. You notice how the planks underfoot provide a stable path forward while offering scenic views of the river below. You take a deep breath and inhale the fresh air.

Consider the support systems you have in your life—friends, family, or mentors who can provide guidance and comfort during times of transition. Recognize and feel gratitude for the connection and love that surrounds you, knowing that you don't have to navigate these changes alone. The bridge represents not only the path forward, but also the support and strength that others offer you as you move through life's transitions.

As you start walking across the bridge, offer compassion to yourself, acknowledging the courage it takes to face change. Recognize each step as an achievement, reinforcing your resilience and commitment to move forward. Silently encourage yourself by saying, "I am capable and strong. I can handle this change."

See yourself managing this transition by focusing on small steps. Recognize that all transitions begin and end with simple efforts. Reflect on the actions you've taken and those you will take in the future. Embrace the excitement about the possibilities ahead, including the new experiences and opportunities this change will bring. Like a bridge, this transition is a passage to new beginnings, growth, and discovery. As you continue, you reach the center of the bridge, a midpoint where you can look back at where you started and forward to where you're heading.

Continue walking as you grasp the handrail, feeling more confident with each step. Envision the opportunities this change will bring and the gifts it may offer. See the future clearly, filled with potential and promise. Acknowledge that while your life may be different, there will be positive aspects and new experiences. Look back at how far you've come and smile. Recognize that you have successfully managed changes before and will continue to do so in the future. You are nearly at the end of the bridge.

When you are ready, step off the bridge and enter a meadow filled with wildflowers. You glance over to your left and see a monarch butterfly. The future has so many possibilities. You will navigate this transition just like you walked across this bridge— slowly and steadily. Now it's time to return to your current environment. Take these feelings into your day or evening and know you can handle whatever comes your way.

Meditation Journey Twenty-Three: Time-Travel Railway

Take a deep breath, inhale slowly and deeply, and then exhale gently. Let each breath relax your body, releasing any feelings of tension you might be holding. As you breathe more deeply, let your shoulders drop and allow your body to become limp. Continue this calming breathing, feeling yourself becoming more present and centered.

Now, imagine stepping into a grand, old train station. The architecture is a mesmerizing blend of historical grandeur and fantastical whimsy. The station is expansive, echoing with the soft murmurs of countless travelers. It features soaring arches that reach toward a high, vaulted ceiling adorned with frescoes depicting mythical creatures and celestial maps. The walls have a golden hue, casting a warm, inviting glow throughout the space, creating a sense of enchantment that fills the air.

As you walk along the wide, polished marble floors, you notice delicate veins of brown, rust, and crimson shimmering underfoot, adding to the station's ambiance. The wall on one side of the station displays a series of large brass and copper clocks. Their faces are ornate, decorated with symbols and numbers from various eras, each clock ticking in perfect harmony yet showing a different time. These clocks suggest there are many destinations or eras one could journey to from this station.

At the center of the station stands a massive departure board, clacking and whirring as it updates with names of destinations that seem fantastical, such as "Tomorrow's Hopes," "Yesterday's Dreams," and "Adventures Unknown." As you look through the glass windows in the ceiling, the sky shifts in color from dawn to dusk and back again, irrespective of the actual time of day, adding to the station's charm. This is no ordinary train station—it's a hub for time-traveling trains, each destined for distinct moments of transition in your life. It's a place where the boundaries of time and reality blur, offering adventurers the ride of a lifetime.

As you stroll along the platform, you notice many trains, each one labeled with various aspects of life such as "Career," "Love Relationships," "Residence," "Health," "Family," and many other names. Each train car is uniquely designed to take you to a place that will help you with the transition for that life area. You feel drawn to the specific car that corresponds with the change you are currently facing or expecting soon. With curiosity and a sense of readiness, you step aboard this car, finding a comfortable seat beside a large window, preparing for a journey to this aspect of your life.

The train's engine comes to life and hums. The doors close, and the train slowly departs the station. As you peer out the window, the scenery changes from the magical train station to idyllic pastoral landscapes with wide green meadows. You enter a dark tunnel. As you come out, you arrive at a stop with the sign, "Welcome to Transitions Station."

This is your destination, so you get off the train. When you alight, you meet a compassionate being who tells you they will show you this part of your life. They lead you to an ethereal garden filled with many reflective pools. They guide you to one that is oblong, its surface smooth and mirror-like. The being gestures for you to gaze into the water, where vivid images of your past unfold related to this transition.

First, you see the beginning of this phase of your life. The water reveals key moments, the people involved, and the initial steps that set this part of your life in motion. You witness the excitement, uncertainties, and hopes that accompanied the start. These scenes play out like a movie, displaying the people who have been part of these experiences, the discussions you've had, the emotions you felt, and the key memories.

As the images shift, you move into the middle of this phase. You see yourself navigating through significant events, facing challenges, and celebrating. This period of growth and learning is filled with highs and lows, painting a complex picture of your experiences and emotions.

Finally, the pool shows the most recent part of this phase, bringing you to the present. You see how everything has come together, the culmination of your efforts, and the changes you've undergone. As you watch, you feel a deep sense of nostalgia mixed with contemplation of the impact of the upcoming transition. Acknowledge these emotions, whether they are sadness, frustration, fear, excitement, or a blend of all these feelings. These emotions are a natural and integral part of your personal growth and adaptation process.

As you continue watching, the scenery transforms, vividly depicting the major change you are about to undertake. Each scene unfolds in vibrant detail, showing the outcomes you hope for and the challenges you fear. The compassionate being reminds you that all change is difficult and that you need to be gentle with yourself as you navigate this transition. As you contemplate the future, the being surrounds you with a golden light of compassion that immediately calms your nerves and allows you to breathe deeply.

This golden light acts as a nurturing force, strengthening your spirit and helping you accept and embrace the challenges of this transition. The light fills every part of your being, soothing your mind and heart. You consciously release any self-judgment or criticism, replacing it with acceptance and understanding. Remind yourself that you can navigate life's changes with grace and courage. You acknowledge it is okay to have moments of struggle and that you deserve kindness, especially from yourself. As you continue to breathe in this golden light, you feel hopeful.

The reflective pool shows you successfully navigating this transition. You see yourself thriving, enjoying life, forging better relationships, or perhaps experiencing improved health. These positive images fill you with determination. You envision the new environments you will inhabit, the new people you will meet, and the new routines you will establish. You see yourself adapting, overcoming obstacles with a calm demeanor, and growing more confident.

The compassionate being leads you back to the train, and you board. You travel back to the station, and the train slows, signaling the end of your journey. As it comes to a gentle stop, you prepare to disembark, feeling refreshed and empowered. Step off the train and take a moment to feel the firm floor beneath your feet. Now come back to your current environment, knowing that you can manage this current transition.

Meditation Journey Twenty-Four: The Movie of Your Life

Begin by finding a quiet, comfortable space where you can fully relax and focus. Once you're settled, start by taking deep, slow breaths. Inhale deeply through your nose, filling your lungs with air, and exhale slowly several times. With each breath, feel yourself descending into a deeper state of relaxation. Allow your muscles to loosen, and your mind to become calm.

Now, imagine being ushered into a private movie theater where you are the only ticket holder. The theater is luxurious and intimate, designed for the ultimate viewing experience. You sink into a plush burgundy seat that envelops you in comfort. In your hand, you hold a drink and a box of popcorn, the familiar, buttery scent adding to the cozy ambiance. Take a few deep breaths, feeling the plush seat supporting you, and allow yourself to fully settle in for the experience.

As the lights dim and the big screen flickers to life, you see the movie of your life. This film is a montage of pivotal moments—major changes in career, relationships, living situations, and significant shifts in your beliefs and perspectives. These are the moments when you experienced the most significant growth—the defining points of your life that have shaped who you are today.

The movie begins with scenes from your early childhood. You see yourself as a child, filled with innocence and curiosity, exploring the world with wide-eyed wonder. You watch as you experience the joy of discovering new things, delighting in small adventures, and savoring the first moments of independence. There are scenes of you playing and making friends, including your first day of school—a day filled with a mix of nerves and excitement. You see yourself at home playing, out in the neighborhood with friends, perhaps running or bicycling, playing games, and laughing. The film captures these early memories, which built the foundations of trust and friendship, contributing to your early sense of identity and belonging.

The scenes then transition to your adolescence, a time of change and discovery. You see yourself engaging in various activities, meeting new people, and exploring your interests. See the friends who were significant during these years, with whom you shared many important moments. See the adults who influenced and shaped your adolescence. Recall the pivotal moments, the words exchanged, and the emotions you felt. You remember the people you had crushes on or were romantically involved with as a teenager. You also recall the activities you loved during that time and the many mistakes you made. All these experiences contributed to the person you are today.

The movie shows your years at school and the many places you learned. You see teachers who were important to you and others who influenced you in small and large ways. These years were crucial in your development.

Next, the movie shows your transition into adulthood and the world of work. You see yourself on the first days at your job, grappling with the steep learning curve and meeting new colleagues. The scenes depict your growth in this new environment, highlighting the challenges you overcame and the satisfaction of your achievements. You see mentors who guided you, peers who supported you, and the moments that defined your career path. The movie shows the twists and turns of your professional journey, including opportunities and obstacles. You watch yourself aspire for better positions, perhaps changing companies or even careers, and continuously adapt to new environments. Notice the evolution of your skills, the deepening of your professional identity, and the development of your confidence.

The focus then shifts to the various relationships in your life—romantic partnerships, friendships, and family. You see key moments that brought joy, such as meeting your partner, dating, weddings, and children. You witness how your family life evolved and you see the friendships that were almost like family to you. There are also scenes where relationships changed, with some ending or evolving in unexpected ways. All these relationships have taught you important lessons about love, loss, forgiveness, and growth, contributing to your emotional development.

Interspersed throughout the movie are moments of leisure and personal interests—activities that have brought joy and fulfillment. You see hobbies that have become passions, vacations that provided rest and adventure, and simple pleasures like watching a favorite TV show or reading a book. You recognize the significance of these moments, appreciating how they have contributed to your overall well-being and happiness.

As the movie continues, you reflect on all the transitions you have experienced. Each scene, each memory, is a testament to your resilience and growth. You see the challenges you faced, the successes and failures, and how each change has sculpted you into the person you are today. You feel grateful for the journey, for the lessons learned, and the strength gained. The difficulties you faced as a child or adolescent are integral parts of your unique story, giving you a distinctive sensitivity and understanding. The challenges of adulthood—whether in work, family, or health—have not been easy, but you have risen to meet them, each obstacle contributing to your character.

Now, the screen shifts to a preview of the future, offering glimpses of a significant transition you currently face. These scenes are not fully clear, more like fragments or foreshadowing of what's to come. As you watch, feel a sense of confidence growing within you. Given all that you have been through, you trust in your ability to handle whatever the future holds. You welcome this new phase as an opportunity for further growth and discovery. The anticipation of future adventures fills you with hope and excitement.

As the movie draws to a close, the lights in the theater gradually brighten. You feel a deep sense of gratitude and self-compassion. It dawns on you that you're the director of your own story, capable of navigating each transition with grace and strength. You have the wisdom and resilience to face any challenge that comes your way.

When you're ready, gently rise from your seat. Come back to your current environment, carrying these feelings with you into the day or evening.

Chapter 8: Embracing Your Parenting Journey

Now I turn to a role that brings immense joy and frustration: parenting. For many, this is one of the most significant and defining aspects of life. It's a journey filled with highs and lows, moments of joy and sadness, and endless opportunities for growth and reflection.

Parenting is an incredibly complex task. There are no perfect guidelines or manuals for raising children, and what works for one child and one family may not work for another. Most parents strive to do their best and to make good decisions for their children. However, it's common for parents to look back and feel they could have done things differently or done more.

Parenting is a learning process, and each stage brings new challenges and opportunities. It's a journey that evolves as both you and your child grow and change. Many parents experience self-doubt and guilt, questioning their choices and worrying about the impact they have on their children. These feelings are normal but can be overwhelming. And as time passes, perspectives on parenting can shift. In hindsight, parents may look back and regret some of their actions, which may have been perceived more positively in that time period.

This chapter delves into the importance of recognizing and embracing your efforts as a parent. It doesn't matter if you are currently raising young ones or if your children have left the nest. Many people undervalue and doubt their parenting because it's challenging work, and no one gets it perfectly right. No one has all the answers.

Although perfection in parenting is unattainable, most parents do the best they can with the resources, knowledge, and circumstances at their disposal. It's vital to acknowledge the love and effort that informed your parenting choices, even if some decisions might seem flawed in retrospect. Reflecting on your parenting journey offers a chance for personal growth and can enhance your relationships with your children, no matter their age.

Embracing self-compassion is important. This means forgiving yourself for past mistakes and understanding that parenting involves continuous learning and adapting. Through this perspective, you can see each step in your parenting history not just as a challenge, but as an opportunity for personal development.

The meditation journeys in this chapter will give you a healthy perspective on this part of life. They will offer support, encourage reflection, and foster a sense of peace and acceptance about parenting.

The experience of parenting is uniquely personal. It has moments of love, joy, and triumph, along with challenges and opportunities for learning. Approaching this experience with kindness and understanding towards yourself is just as important as the love and guidance you give to your children.

**Meditation Journey Twenty-Five: The Hall of Happy
Memories**

Find a quiet, comfortable space where you can sit undisturbed.
Begin by taking deep, slow breaths. As you breathe in, feel a wave
of relaxation spreading through your body. It starts at the top of your
head, moves down to your face, neck, and upper shoulders. Let your
shoulders drop, feeling them become heavy and relaxed. Then, let
this relaxing energy flow down your body to your arms, torso,
thighs, calves, and finally, your feet. Release any tension and feel
the support of the ground beneath you. Take a few slow breaths, each
one bringing you deeper into a state of calm.

Now, close your eyes and imagine yourself stepping into The
Hall of Happy Memories, a special space floating in another realm.

This majestic hall is adorned in gleaming marble, its surfaces polished to a perfect sheen that reflects the soft glow of sunlight streaming through the high, arched windows. The light creates a warm and inviting atmosphere, casting golden hues throughout the space. The architecture of the hall is grand, with a vaulted ceiling that curves gracefully overhead. Elegant chandeliers hang from the ceiling, their crystals shimmering and refracting the light, adding to the hall's elegant beauty.

As you admire this space, you notice the hall is lined with square stone planters filled with beautiful white roses and gardenias. The roses, with their velvety white petals, emit a sweet fragrance reminiscent of honey and citrus, while the gardenias, with their star-shaped blossoms, add a blended scent of coconut and jasmine to the air. The combined fragrances that fill the hall create a pleasant aroma.

Lining the walls are special windows; they don't look outward but serve as portals to beautiful scenes of your life, like snapshots from a movie. These glowing windows depict moments from your parenting journey, each one showcasing different stages and experiences. As you prepare to walk down the hall, you feel a sense of anticipation and warmth, eager to relive your most cherished memories.

You approach the first window and admire the floral arrangement, gently touching the soft petals of the rose. The scent becomes stronger but remains pleasant and not overpowering. Through the window, you see the everyday acts of care and love you provided for your children—moments of ensuring their safety, feeding them, holding them close, and comforting them when they were upset. You see yourself in those countless, often unnoticed moments of vigilance and tenderness: securing a car seat, preparing meals, soothing nighttime fears, and tending to scraped knees. These foundational acts formed the bedrock of your relationship with your children, grounded in your unwavering focus on their well-being.

As you move from window to window, each memory comes alive with vivid clarity. The joy, the pride, and the love you felt for them are clear. The windows show simple yet profound memories—teaching them how to tie their shoes, how to cross a street safely, and how to dress themselves. Each act of love and kindness is highlighted, reminding you of the impact you have had on their lives through these small, everyday actions.

The next set of windows highlights your efforts in fostering your children's emotional and personal growth. You see the times when you encouraged them, celebrated their achievements, and supported their interests. These scenes depict moments driving them to activities, cheering them on at events, praising their efforts, and helping with homework. You remember listening attentively to their concerns and dreams, always there to offer a comforting word or a gentle nudge in the right direction. These moments helped to build their self-esteem and independence, and the windows show them blossoming under your guidance and affirmation.

Further down the hall, the windows depict joyous times spent together in play and relaxation. You see vacations, playdates, games, and simple afternoons or evenings spent watching TV or movies together. The images capture laughter and love. You see holidays and birthdays where you tried to find just the right gift. You see them thrilled with your attention and love, and you also see the quiet contentment of simply being together. These joyful moments created a strong bond.

As you continue down the hall, you encounter windows that showcase significant milestones and major events in your children's lives. You see graduations, family weddings, and other grand celebrations. These are the standout chapters in your shared story, marked by joy and personal achievements. Each major event

118

celebrated in The Hall of Happy Memories highlights your role in these significant moments, cementing your place in these moments of their lives.

In the last section of the hall, the windows reflect times when you went above and beyond for your children, putting their needs ahead of your own. You see yourself staying up all night comforting them during illnesses, spending countless hours helping them with school projects, and sacrificing personal ambitions to attend their events. These scenes capture the countless ways you prioritized their happiness and growth, even at your own expense. They reveal the deep love that motivated your actions and the sacrifices you made for their well-being.

At the end of the hall, you reach the last window, where several phrases appear, encapsulating your parenting experience:

"I shared many loving moments with them."

"I created special memories."

"I expressed my love in so many ways as a parent."

These words resonate with the pride and fulfillment you feel, affirming the importance of your journey.

Spend a few more moments basking in the glow of your memories, appreciating the beauty and joy that these experiences brought into your life. Acknowledge the effort, love, and dedication you poured into raising children. You have played a crucial role in shaping their lives and in creating a tapestry of beautiful memories.

Now, it's time to leave The Hall of Happy Memories. When you are ready, come back to your present environment.

Meditation Journey Twenty-Six: The Celestial Realm

Choose a secluded spot where you can relax undisturbed. Make yourself comfortable, settling into a position where you can remain still and at ease. Start by breathing slowly. Inhale deeply, filling your lungs fully and allowing your body to relax. As you exhale, release any tension or stress. With each breath, feel your muscles loosening and your mind clearing. Let your shoulders drop. Feel the weight of the world lift from them, allowing your body to sink into the surface where you're sitting. Take several deep breaths, each one bringing you into a state of tranquility.

Now, imagine a celestial realm, a dimension beyond our own, where the essence of love and acceptance permeates every part of this world. You find yourself transported to this ethereal place, where the sky paints a magnificent tapestry of colors, blending the most beautiful sunsets and sunrises you've ever seen. The sky shifts from vibrant blues to glowing golds, soft pinks, and deep purples, creating a mesmerizing and ever-changing scene. Dominating the sky is a large, glowing orb resembling a moon, casting a gentle, silver light across the landscape. The ground beneath your feet feels solid and secure, yet you sense the laws of physics are different here.

The landscapes are dynamic, constantly transforming. One moment, towering mountains surround you, their peaks piercing the sky; the next, you find yourself in vast, flat plains that stretch endlessly in every direction. Lush forests give way to serene deserts, each new scene more breathtaking than the last. Despite the shifting surroundings, you feel firmly rooted to the ground, a quiet observer of this ever-changing beauty. This realm exudes a sense of peace and wonder.

As you marvel at this extraordinary world, a wise, luminous being approaches. This being embodies universal wisdom and unconditional love, radiating a soft, glowing light. They greet you warmly. Their presence is soothing and comforting. This being has an aura of deep understanding, and they seem to know all the intricacies of your life and experiences. They explain this realm is a place of reflection and healing, where you can explore and gain insights into your journey as a parent.

The wise being guides you to a specific area of this celestial realm, dedicated to parenting. As you walk together, you feel as if everything is exactly as it should be and that everything will work out in the end. A strong sense of contentment washes over you. You accept you're here for a reason, that all things are as they are meant to be. Though you're not entirely sure why, you feel ready to embrace your life as it is.

Above, the sky bursts with colors—bright oranges and yellows transition into captivating blues and greens. It's as if the universe is celebrating your presence, putting on a spectacular display just for you. A calmness settles within you, along with an eagerness to follow the luminous being. You are confident that it will be a wonderful experience.

The luminous being guides you into a surreal garden, unlike anything you've seen before. It's filled with silver flowers and foliage that glow softly in the ambient light. The plants seem to sway gently, as if in rhythm with the cosmic energies of this realm. At the center of the garden stands a sparkling fountain, its waters constantly shifting through a mesmerizing array of colors. Initially, the water flows with a soothing light blue hue reminiscent of a serene lake. This calming blue gradually transitions to a bold and vibrant red, evoking the color of a blooming rose. The red then softens into a refreshing green, like the lush leaves of a thriving garden. As the green fades, the water turns a warm orange, glowing with the energy of a brilliant sunrise. Finally, the fountain's waters deepen into a rich, velvety black, like the mysterious depths of a starry night sky.

The luminous being conveys a deep understanding and empathy for you as a parent without saying a word. They acknowledge both the joys and challenges that come with raising a child. This being knows the depth of your love, the fears you have faced, and the hopes you hold for your child's future. There's no judgment here; instead, you feel completely accepted for all your efforts, both the triumphs and the times when you felt you fell short.

As you stand together, the being shows you vivid images of your parenting journey. See the moment you first became a parent, feeling a mix of anticipation, excitement, and perhaps nervousness. The images flow seamlessly, showing you the significant moments that shaped your experience: first steps, first words, first birthdays. You see the milestones of your child's life—starting school, making friends, and growing into their own person. Each image stirs a deep sense of love within you.

The luminous being shows you the immense effort you have poured into parenting. Whether comforting a crying child, attending school events, providing guidance, or simply being present, every action was part of your commitment to your child's well-being. The luminous being helps you see these moments contributing to your child's development.

You also see moments when you felt you could have done better—times when you raised your voice, missed an important event, or weren't as patient or understanding as you wished to be. The luminous being gently reminds you that parenting is a continuous learning experience filled with opportunities for growth. They encourage you to forgive yourself for any perceived shortcomings, understanding that you made the best decisions you could with the knowledge and resources available at the time.

This wise being helps you view your past with compassion, showing you that your efforts were sincere, even in moments of self-doubt. They remind you that perfection is unattainable and that what matters most is your genuine love and commitment. This luminous being encourages you to practice self-compassion, to recognize that learning comes from every experience, and to embrace the present moment as an opportunity to continue becoming the best version of yourself.

They guide you to see the challenges you face in parenting not as insurmountable obstacles, but as opportunities to create a deeper connection with your child. You are reminded that every obstacle you encounter is a chance to understand your child better and to grow as a parent. If your child is an adult, they encourage you to embrace this new phase of your relationship, offering support and understanding as your child navigates their own path. They remind you that your role as a parent evolves, and that you will always offer love and wisdom. Being a parent is a lifetime job.

Finally, the luminous being presents you with a gift, a symbol of your strengths and the positive impact you have had on your child's life. This gift embodies the love, dedication, and resilience you have shown throughout your parenting journey. As you accept this gift, repeat these affirmations silently to yourself:

"Love has guided my parenting journey."

"I embrace the good and bad moments with compassion and understanding."

"I honor the effort I have put into nurturing and supporting my family."

"I am grateful for the bond with my child and the lessons we have learned."

Spend a few more moments in this realm, basking in the unconditional love and acceptance that surrounds you. Allow this experience to fill you with confidence and peace, knowing that you have been a loving parent.

Now it's time to leave this realm. Come back to your present environment, taking these feelings into your day or evening.

Meditation Journey Twenty-Seven: The Ancient Grove

Find a quiet and comfortable place where you can sit undisturbed. As you settle into your chosen spot, close your eyes and take several slow, deep breaths. With each inhalation, feel a sense of calmness entering your body, filling your lungs, and spreading throughout your being. As you exhale, release any worries, letting them flow out of you with each exhalation. Allow each breath to bring you into a greater state of peacefulness.

Now, imagine yourself stepping into a serene, ancient grove, a place where time seems to stand still, and nature's wisdom permeates the air. This sacred grove, a hidden gem in the heart of a timeless forest, is home to towering trees that have seen countless generations. These majestic trees embody strength, resilience, and the interconnectedness of all life. As you step into the grove, it feels as if you are entering a grand cathedral.

The air in the grove is cool and moist, carrying the rich, earthy scent of moss and soil that blankets the forest floor. You fill your lungs with this fresh air. Above you, the thick canopy of lush green leaves filters sunlight into dappled shapes that dance playfully along the ground. These warm, golden spots illuminate the grove. You absorb the calmness of the environment and let it infuse every part of you.

The trees surrounding you are grand sentinels, their trunks wide and gnarled, bearing the marks of time. Their bark forms intricate, lacy patterns, telling a story of survival, growth, and the wisdom gained from living through countless seasons. Some of these trees are hundreds of years old. Their branches stretch high above, touching the sky, creating a natural cathedral of green. As you walk deeper into the grove, you notice how quiet it is here. There are only a few muted sounds, enhancing the stillness. Yet you feel deeply connected to this secluded place and the vast web of life it sustains.

As you venture further, you discover a weathered flat stone, perfectly positioned for sitting. You take a seat, feeling the coolness of the stone beneath you. The ancient trees form a protective circle around this spot, creating a natural sanctuary where you can reflect and find peace. In this quiet, sacred space, you think of your child. In your mind's eye, you see their face, recalling their smile, the twinkle in their eyes, and their unique expressions. You reflect on the things that bring them joy—their passions, hobbies, and favorite activities. As you sit, you send thoughts of love and positive energy towards them, wishing them happiness and fulfillment in all they do.

Next, you contemplate the challenges your child faces—the difficulties they encounter and the obstacles they must overcome. You reflect on what you've seen them struggle with, and the frustrations and worries they've expressed. With compassion and empathy, you send them thoughts of strength. Visualize them navigating these challenges with determination. With each breath in, draw positivity and warmth from the grove's tranquil energy. As you exhale, imagine sending this supportive energy to your child, enveloping them, and giving them courage. See them successfully overcoming their struggles, empowered by your unwavering love and support.

As you continue to breathe deeply, take a moment to reflect on the gratitude you feel for being a part of your child's life. Think about how much you have grown personally through your experiences with them.

Feel a sense of pride in their accomplishments, both big and small, and envision them achieving their dreams and aspirations. With each exhale, release any worries you may have about their future, trusting in their abilities and the support system that surrounds them. Acknowledge the potential that lies within them, confident that they will navigate life's journey with strength and grace. Allow yourself to feel a deep sense of peace, knowing that they are a resilient and capable individual.

You also consider the bond you share with your child, a connection forged through shared experiences and deep affection. This bond is a testament to the countless moments that have brought you closer—each one adding to your relationship. Recall the special moments you've shared: the laughter that bubbled up during joyful times, the tears shed during moments of vulnerability, and the quiet, comforting silences where no words were needed to express understanding and love.

Picture this connection as a strong, unbreakable rope that binds you both, woven from the fibers of trust, respect, and unconditional love. This rope, though invisible, is powerful and enduring, capable of withstanding any challenge life may throw your way. As you visualize this, feel the warmth and energy of your love flowing through this bond. Imagine this energy traveling along the rope, enveloping your child with a sense of security and belonging. This bond is a source of strength for both of you, a reminder that you are never truly alone, as your hearts are forever intertwined.

The ancient grove has provided a space for reflection and peace. Now it's time to leave this sanctuary. Slowly rise from the flat stone and begin your journey back through the grove. When you are ready, come back to your current environment, taking these feelings into your day or evening.

Chapter 9: Navigating Grief and Loss

Grief is a profound experience. It's a journey we all embark on in our lives, yet it remains one of the most challenging paths to navigate. When we lose someone we love, whether it's the result of death or because the relationship has ended, it can feel as if the world has shifted beneath our feet.

Grief is an emotional response to loss, and it knows no bounds. It doesn't adhere to timelines or follow a predictable pattern. Instead, grief is a complex and often overwhelming mix of emotions—sadness, anger, confusion, and even moments of numbness. It can leave us feeling adrift in a sea of uncertainty, desperately trying to make sense of our world that has changed irrevocably.

The Myth of "Doing Grief Right"

There is no correct way to grieve. Each person's experience with grief is unique and deeply personal. The myth that there is a correct way to grieve can lead to feelings of inadequacy and self-judgment. And you may wonder whether you're doing it right. If you compare your grieving journey to others, you might feel that you should be further along or less affected. You might even hide your feelings, fearing that your authentic emotions are somehow inappropriate.

One of the most challenging emotions that often goes with grief is guilt. You may feel guilty for things left unsaid or undone, for past moments of anger or frustration, or for simply surviving when your loved one did not. Guilt can be a heavy burden, adding to the already overwhelming emotions of grief.

It's crucial to recognize that guilt is a natural reaction, but it's not a reflection of your worthiness or your love for the person you have lost. In fact, it often stems from the depth of your love and your desire for things to be different.

Embracing Self-Compassion in Grief

So, where does self-compassion fit into this complex landscape of grief and loss? Self-compassion offers a lifeline. A way to navigate the turbulent waters of grief with greater understanding and kindness toward yourself.

In the pages that follow, there are meditations that honor your grief journey and allow space for all the messy, complicated emotions that accompany it. Through self-compassion, you'll discover that you are grieving in your own way, on your own timeline, and there is no need to carry the weight of guilt.

Remember that your grief is a testament to the love you hold in your heart. It's a natural response to loss. And in embracing self-compassion, you'll find the strength and resilience to navigate the path of grief with greater grace and understanding.

Meditation Journey Twenty-Eight: Releasing Grief in the Crystal Healing House

Find a quiet and comfortable space where you won't be disturbed. Take a moment to settle into your surroundings, feeling the stability and support of the ground beneath you. Begin by taking deep, slow breaths to center yourself. Inhale deeply through your nose, allowing your chest and abdomen to rise as you fill your lungs with air. Hold for a moment, then exhale slowly and fully, releasing any tightness in your muscles. Repeat this process, taking several deep, purposeful breaths, each one bringing you deeper into a state of calm and relaxation.

Imagine yourself walking along a tranquil path leading to the Crystal Healing House, a sanctuary crafted entirely from radiant healing crystals, designed specifically for those who are grieving. As you draw closer, the house shimmers in the sunlight, displaying a spectrum of colors. The roof is a blend of deep purple and blue crystals that sparkle under the sun, while the second-floor glows warmly with yellow, green, and deep crimson crystals. As you get closer, the house becomes even more enchanting with its dazzling display of light and color. The path is lined with small white quartz stones that crunch softly underfoot. The front porch, supported by columns encrusted with pink and purple crystals, invites you to pause and admire the house's beautiful facade.

Come inside the open front door of the Crystal Healing House. As you step inside, you're enveloped by a soothing atmosphere. The walls, made of translucent quartz, diffuse a soft, healing light that immediately puts you at ease. As you breathe in, the air calms you even more deeply. The space feels serene, a perfect environment for reflection and healing.

You wander through this healing haven, your fingers brushing against the smooth crystal walls and doorways. The cool sensation of the crystals against your skin is soothing. Each room you enter has a unique energy and light, influenced by the different crystals that make up the walls and floors. You notice that each room has its own distinct color.

You feel drawn to a room where deep red garnets line the walls and floors, a stone known for helping to manage intense emotions of sorrow. The rich red hues of the garnets imbue the room with vibrant and intense energy. Entering the room, you touch the many garnets embedded in the walls, feeling them absorbing your feelings of loss. Allow yourself to fully experience these intense feelings of sadness, knowing that the room draws them out and provides a safe space for release. The energy in the room helps to dissipate your sorrow, leaving you with a profound sense of relief.

Next, you move into a room specifically designed for releasing guilt. The walls of the room, made entirely of rose quartz, cast a soft pink light throughout the space. Rose quartz is renowned for its heart-healing properties, and this room contains a warm, comforting energy. As you touch the rose quartz stones, you focus on taking deep, cleansing breaths. With each exhale, you bring any lingering feelings of guilt to the surface—regrets about things said or unsaid, actions taken or not taken. The rose quartz gently absorbs these feelings, transforming them into forgiveness and self-compassion. You feel a weight lift from your shoulders, replaced by a sense of peace and acceptance.

You take another deep breath and proceed to a room crafted entirely of clear crystal, designed to enhance clarity and insight. As you enter this room, you reflect on your loss and its deeper significance. You touch the clear crystals, recalling major memories and the many things you gained from this relationship. As you reflect, you feel a deep sense of gratitude for all that this individual brought into your life—their kindness, wisdom, and the unique experiences you shared. This room, with its pure, clear energy, helps you to honor and appreciate the lasting influence of them in your life.

Next, you enter a room with walls and floors made of emerald, a stone associated with love. The rich green hues fill the space with nurturing energy, enveloping you in a warm embrace. In this room, you sense the presence of the person you are grieving. You feel a strong sense of their love, which seems eternal and transcends the boundaries of physical presence. As you stand there, you hear this person speaking to you. You hear their voice, filled with love, forgiveness, and reassurance, reminding you they are still with you in spirit. They express deep affection, forgive any misunderstandings or unresolved issues, and say that they are at peace. Their words resonate within you, offering comfort and solace. This conversation feels wondrous and healing.

Finally, you make your way to the central meditation room at the heart of the house. This room is constructed from large amethyst crystals, known for their balancing properties. At the center of the room, there is a massive amethyst crystal that fills the room with a soft purple light. You touch this enormous amethyst, which calms your mind and opens your heart. As you absorb this energy, you close your eyes and silently repeat these affirmations:

"I acknowledge my grief with tenderness and love."

"I allow myself to mourn and to heal at my own pace."

"I embrace my heart with compassion."

"I am not alone. I am surrounded by the healing energies of the universe."

Spend as much time as you need in this healing sanctuary, letting the crystals cleanse, heal, and uplift you. Whenever you feel overwhelmed by grief, remember that the Crystal Healing House is here for you to release those powerful emotions.

When you feel ready, come back to your current environment. Take these feelings with you into your day or evening.

Meditation Journey Twenty-Nine: Deep Connections at the Crystal Fountain

Find a quiet and comfortable place where you can sit down. Close your eyes and begin by taking a few deep breaths to center yourself. Inhale deeply, allowing your chest and abdomen to rise as you fill your lungs with air. Hold this breath for a moment, then exhale slowly. Repeat this process, taking several deep, purposeful breaths. As you breathe in, feel a sense of calm entering your body. As you exhale, let go of any stress, allowing your shoulders to drop and your body to relax. Continue breathing deeply and rhythmically.

Now, imagine yourself in a serene valley bathed in the soft, golden light of the sun. Gentle hills encircle this valley, which isolates it from the outside world. The air is fresh, filled with the sweet fragrance of wildflowers that blanket the grassy valley floor. These yellow flowers sway gently in a light breeze, adding a touch of color and movement to the tranquil scene. The entire valley is lush and beautiful, a perfect place for reflection and healing.

In the center of the valley, you see a dazzling crystal fountain. This masterpiece of craftsmanship features sparkling water flowing gracefully from a series of crystal bowls, each slightly larger than the last, stacked above one another. The smallest bowl overflows into the next, and this cascading effect continues until the water descends into a large crystal pool. The water catches the sunlight, creating a beautiful display of light and color. This fountain occupies a sacred space where souls can connect across time and space— whether they have passed on or are simply distant. It is a place of reconnection for hearts that have been separated.

As you get closer to the fountain, you notice how the crystal glistens under the sun's warm rays. The sound of cascading water soothes you. You see intricate flowers and vines delicately etched into the crystal, adding to the fountain's ethereal beauty. You feel a deep sense of peace in this beautiful place and breathe in the fresh air.

Place your hand into the water, which is surprisingly warm. Moving your hand back-and-forth feels soothing. As you experience the sight, sound and feel of this fountain, you think about your loved one—the person you have lost or are separated from. Emotions rise within you, and you allow yourself to feel them freely, knowing that you are in a sacred space where you can safely explore these feelings.

When you look up from the water, you see your loved one standing before you. They appear as you remember them, with all their unique qualities and expressions. You notice the details of their face, their smile, the way they hold themselves, and the clothing they wore. Every subtle gesture and expression is familiar to you, bringing a sense of warmth and comfort. They look at you with a smile that reaches their eyes, a look filled with tremendous affection and reassurance. It feels as though no time has passed, and you reunite with them once more.

You smile and embrace them. Starting a heartfelt conversation, you express the feelings and thoughts that you've been carrying. You tell them what they meant to you, how they influenced your life, and how their presence made a difference. You speak of the void their absence has left and how it has affected you. As you share these intimate reflections, you feel a release, as if a burden is being lifted from your heart.

You recount specific treasured memories about them, moments that brought you joy and that you cherish. These are the experiences and moments of deep connection. You express your gratitude for these times, thanking them for being a part of your life and for the memories you created together. As you reminisce, you feel comforted that these memories will always be a part of you.

You also take this opportunity to say anything that has been left unsaid or is unresolved. If there were misunderstandings or regrets, you acknowledge them and, if needed, offer an apology. You explain your feelings and intentions, letting them know that you never meant to hurt them. Your loved one listens with compassion and understanding. They reassure you they are at peace and that they care for you deeply. They tell you they understand your feelings and that, while they cannot be with you physically, their spirit remains connected to yours. And they remind you that love transcends all boundaries. The bond you share will never be broken.

As your conversation draws to a close, your loved one extends their hand toward you, holding a symbolic gift—a token of love or wisdom. This gift might take any form: a flower, a crystal, or another meaningful object. You accept this gift with gratitude, recognizing it as a symbol of your ongoing connection. This token serves as a reminder that the love you shared continues to live on in your heart, guiding and comforting you in times of need.

It's almost time to leave the crystal fountain and return to the present. You take a moment to express any final thoughts or feelings to your loved one. You might share a last message of love, hope, or gratitude, knowing that this moment of connection will remain with you. As you prepare to depart, your loved one smiles at you. Their presence is still warm and reassuring. They tell you how much they love you and how that will always be the case. You know that while this visit is ending, the bond you share endures.

Now, it's time to leave the crystal fountain. When you feel ready, come back to your present environment. Carry these feelings into your day or evening, knowing that you can return to this serene valley and the crystal fountain whenever you need to reconnect with your loved one.

Meditation Journey Thirty: Releasing Guilt at the Celestial Observatory

Find a quiet and comfortable place where you can take time for yourself. Begin by taking a few deep, cleansing breaths. Inhale deeply through your nose, allowing your chest and abdomen to rise, filling your lungs with air. As you exhale slowly, release any discomfort you may be feeling. Repeat this process several times, focusing on the rhythm of your breath and the sensation of relaxation spreading through your body. Let your shoulders drop, feel your muscles loosen, and continue breathing deeply until you feel fully relaxed and centered.

Now, imagine yourself entering a celestial observatory, a place that offers a panoramic view of the night sky. This observatory is not just for observation but also a place for reflection and release. This majestic structure has high, arching walls made of dark, polished stone, exuding a sense of timelessness and strength. The upper part of the observatory's dome is completely open to the sky, revealing a breathtaking view of the stars and planets. Stars twinkle in the dark sky, creating a serene and wondrous atmosphere.

A metal spiral staircase leads to the upper part of the observatory, and you begin your ascent. The handrail feels cool and sturdy under your grip, the metal smooth but slightly worn from years of use. Each step echoes softly. Upon reaching the top, you step into the open dome, and the view that greets you is breathtaking. The observatory's remote, elevated plateau offers a vantage point unparalleled in its clarity and scope. Here, far from city lights and pollution, the sky is a deep, velvety black, making the stars, planets, and galaxies shine with an extraordinary brightness. You can see the Milky Way, its dense band of stars forming a luminous river across the sky. Nebulae glow in soft hues of pink and purple. As you take in this view, a shooting star streaks across the sky, leaving a brief, dazzling trail.

A sense of awe and wonder fills you. The scale and beauty of the universe are humbling, reminding you of the vastness of existence beyond your everyday experiences. The observatory's unique position and the pristine clarity of the sky make it feel as though you could reach out and touch the stars.

This celestial observatory is unique because it serves as a convergence point for cosmic energies. It provides visitors with a space to reflect on their lives and release pent-up emotions. The atmosphere feels charged with a subtle energy that enhances your sense of connection to the universe and your own thoughts and feelings. As you stand gazing up at the vast expanse of the night sky, you experience both a profound sense of your smallness in the grand scheme of the universe and a deep connection to the greater whole.

In this serene moment, you think about the person you've lost and any guilt you've been carrying about them. Perhaps there are things you didn't say or actions you wish you had taken, moments you now regret. As these thoughts surface, recognize that feelings of guilt are common when someone is no longer in your life. You acknowledge humans are not perfect; we make mistakes, say things we regret, and sometimes fail to act. This realization brings a sense of compassion toward yourself, acknowledging that these are natural feelings.

As you reflect on this guilt, you realize it is not contributing to your current life. Although you have gained wisdom from these experiences, these feelings have become burdens that weigh you down. They cloud your perception of yourself and your past, distorting the reality of your relationship with your loved one. In this celestial observatory, you recognize the need to release these feelings and free yourself from them.

You feel a pulsing energy around you, resonating with the intensity of your emotions. As these feelings of guilt well up inside you, the energy seems to respond, gently pulling these emotions away. It is as if a cloud of dust that has been living within you is being lifted, a cloud that no longer serves any purpose. You see this cloud being extracted from you and sent upward into the vast expanse of space. You watch as this darkness dissipates, merging with the night sky, leaving you feeling lighter and unburdened.

With each breath you take, self-compassion fills the space that guilt once occupied. You forgive yourself for the things you regret, understanding that you did the best you could at the time. As you breathe deeply, you place your hand over your heart. In this sacred space, you say:

"I have made mistakes, but I release this guilt as I take the lessons forward."

"I forgive myself and move forward with strength and grace."

"I will not let my past be defined by guilt, but by the wonderful parts of my relationship with my loved one."

As you repeat these affirmations, feel the truth of them sinking into your soul. Allow peace and acceptance to wash over you, comforting you. This is a place of renewal, and you have allowed yourself to let go of burdens that no longer serve you.

Now, it's time to leave the celestial observatory. Take a moment to appreciate the serene beauty of the night sky one last time. Let the feelings of peace and clarity you have found here sink deeply into your heart. When you are ready, come back to your present environment. And carry these feelings with you into your day or evening.

Chapter 10: Healing from Trauma

Trauma is a haunting and deeply affecting experience that can cast a long shadow over one's life. It comes in many forms, from the wounds of war and violence to the hidden scars of emotional and psychological pain. Everyone's experience with trauma is unique, and the journey to healing is deeply personal.

Feelings of self-blame can sometimes occur after a traumatic event. Even when the trauma is because of circumstances beyond our control, we sometimes blame ourselves and wonder if we could have done something differently or if we were somehow at fault. These thoughts can make the healing process even more challenging.

In this chapter, I want to bring self-compassion to you if you have experienced trauma. Healing from trauma involves recognizing one's inherent worth and resilience. It is about acknowledging the strength it takes to survive and thrive despite the pain. Self-compassion provides a pathway to healing, self-forgiveness, and resilience, and lets you see your journey as unique and valid. It helps in releasing guilt or self-criticism and focuses on nurturing a sense of self-worth and inner strength.

You will find meditation journeys to help you acknowledge your pain, honor your strength, and embrace self-compassion. It is a journey toward self-acceptance, self-kindness, and the reclamation of your narrative. Trauma may have left its mark, but it does not define your worth or potential for healing.

Meditation Journey Thirty-One: The Sunlit Nook

Find a quiet and comfortable space to sit. Take a few moments to settle into a relaxed posture, allowing your body to find a position of ease and comfort. Feel the ground beneath you, providing steady support, and appreciate the safety and serenity of the space you're in. This is your time, a moment for yourself to unwind and let go of any outside concerns. Begin by focusing on your breath, taking slow, deep breaths in through your nose, and exhaling just as slowly. With each breath, feel your body becoming calm. Allow yourself several deep breaths, knowing that you are safe here, in this moment, to take some time for self-care and reflection.

Imagine you are in a cozy, sunlit nook, a personal sanctuary designed for comfort and introspection. This secluded corner has a soft couch with plush cushions, inviting you to sink in and relax. The gentle sunlight streaming through a nearby window bathes the space in a warm, golden glow. This nook is your serene retreat from the world, a place where you are safe. As you continue to take calming breaths, feel the cushions and the ground supporting you fully.

Feel the warmth of the sun on your face and body. This light, originating from a star nearly five billion years old, has traveled across the vast expanse of the universe to reach you. It is infused with the strength and wisdom of countless ages, bringing with it a powerful force of healing and compassion. As the sunlight warms you, it fills you with a deep sense of comfort and peace. You are being cradled in a gentle, nurturing embrace. This ancient light reminds you of the endless cycles of renewal and growth, encouraging you to tap into your own inner strength and resilience.

Now, gently allow your thoughts to turn to the trauma you have endured. Acknowledge its presence in your life without judging yourself. It is natural to feel a range of emotions when reflecting on such experiences. Allow any feelings to surface—whether it's sadness, anger, fear, or confusion. Know that it is okay to feel these emotions; you are in a safe space.

With each breath, draw in the healing rays of the sun, which instill feelings of strength and resilience within you. This light is a source of empowerment, reminding you that you can heal and move beyond this experience. Each breath you take reinforces your inner strength and your belief in your capacity to overcome challenges. The sunlight, with its ancient energy, acts as a reminder that you are part of a larger, enduring universe, and that you too have the capacity for renewal.

If you have been carrying feelings of self-blame or guilt, recognize that these feelings are part of being human, but they are not accurate representations of your worth or character. You are not responsible for what happened to you. With each breath, draw in the sunlight that gently lifts away any heavy layers of self-blame. Visualize this compassionate energy helping you to release this burden, dissolving these feelings into the warmth of the light. As you let go of these feelings, experience the relief and lightness that comes with this release.

You may also carry feelings of shame, which are common among those who have experienced trauma. This emotion can affect one's sense of self, often leading to feelings of being inherently flawed or unworthy of love and connection. Know that these feelings are untrue—you are not flawed, and you are worthy of love and respect. Feel the sunlight as a warm, healing presence that penetrates through any layers of shame, breaking them apart and dissolving them. With each exhale, release the remnants of shame, watching them dissipate into the sunlight.

Now, turn your attention to your wounded self, the part of you that the trauma has affected. See this wounded self as a vulnerable and hurt inner child, deserving of love and understanding. Visualize this small child and reach out to them with compassion, offering comfort and reassurance. Speak gently to this child within you, telling them they are not to blame for what happened, that they are loved and valued. Let them know you understand their feelings and that you are here to support and protect them. Assure this inner child that they are worthy of all the good things in life. As you breathe in the sunlight, imagine wrapping this child in its warm, golden glow, surrounding them with love and safety. This moment of connection is crucial in the healing process, as you acknowledge and nurture the parts of yourself that have hidden in pain and shadow.

As you continue to offer comfort to your inner child, take a moment to reflect on the resilience and courage that have brought you this far. The strength of the sun mirrors your own inner fortitude. With each breath, feel admiration for yourself, acknowledging the bravery and hope that have guided you on your healing journey. Recognize that healing is a gradual process, but you have already made significant progress. Feel proud of yourself for surviving and for the strength you have shown in reaching this point. Understand that each step you take towards healing is an accomplishment, a testament to your determination.

Look ahead to a future where self-compassion guides you through life's ups and downs. Envision yourself returning to this safe nook whenever you need reassurance and strength, knowing that this sunlit sanctuary is always available to you. It reminds you that, despite external challenges, you carry within you a place of profound peace and healing.

As you prepare to leave this nook, feel the warmth and lightness of the sun's rays within you. It's time to return to your present environment, carrying with you the compassion and strength you've cultivated here. Slowly bring your awareness back to your surroundings, feeling the support beneath you. Now, take these feelings into your day or evening.

Meditation Journey Thirty-Two: Healing Cottage

Find a quiet and comfortable place to sit. Take a few deep breaths, allowing your body to relax. Inhale slowly several times. As you exhale, let go of any tension or discomfort you may be holding. This moment is for you, a time to pause and reconnect with yourself. Feel the weight of the world lift from your shoulders, leaving you light and at ease.

Now, close your eyes and imagine walking down a path through a serene forest. With each step, the clear and inviting path connects you more deeply with the natural world. The surrounding forest is teeming with the sounds of nature—the chorus of bird calls, the rustle of leaves swaying in the mild wind, and the soft crackle of leaves and twigs beneath your feet. The sun filters through the trees, casting shadows that dance along the ground.

As you continue along the path, a sense of calm washes over you. You take a deep breath, inhaling the crisp forest air. The invigorating scent of pine needles mingles with the earthy aroma of damp soil and the subtle fragrances of other trees and plants.

You notice the path leads to a sunlit clearing. In the middle of this clearing is a quaint cottage, and you are the only one who has a key to it. The dark green exterior blends seamlessly with the surrounding forest. It feels like this cottage has always been there, waiting for you. The cheery yellow doors and windows create a welcoming feeling. This cottage is not just a structure; it is a sanctuary that only you can access, a place where you are completely safe. This is your special haven, where you can be your true self, free from judgment or expectations.

As you approach the cottage, you take a moment to appreciate its charm. It's large enough to be spacious, but small enough to be cozy. You are completely safe here because you are the only one who can access it. You take the key from your pocket, feeling its reassuring weight in your hand, and unlock the door. The key turns smoothly in the lock, a comforting click signaling the opening of a place where you are truly at home.

As you step inside, a sense of peace instantly settles upon you. The interior of the cottage is warm and inviting, filled with items that bring you joy and comfort. The furniture, soft and plush, beckons you to settle down and unwind. Your shelves are filled with books with stories and knowledge you cherish, alongside your collection of beloved movies and music that resonate with you. Each item in this space reflects your tastes, memories, and passions.

Photographs that capture moments you hold dear, along with keepsakes from your past, are lovingly placed throughout the space, each telling a story of love, laughter, and life. This is your domain, a place where time stands still, allowing you to linger as long as you want. As you move through the rooms, you feel a deep sense of belonging. This is a place where you can truly be yourself, free to explore your thoughts and feelings without fear or hesitation.

Take this moment to experience your personal haven, exploring the various rooms. Each room is specifically designed for you. Perhaps there is a library filled with books that have shaped your thoughts and imagination, a room where you can lose yourself in worlds unknown. Or maybe there's a creative space, where you can write, paint, or craft to your heart's content, letting your creativity flow freely. There's also a cozy bathroom, a sanctuary where you can relax in a warm bath or take a long, soothing shower. This is a place to cleanse not just your body but your mind and spirit as well.

Wander through your quaint cottage, feeling the unique energy of each room. And then, find yourself drawn to the comfortable living room, which offers a stunning view of the forest outside. The large windows allow the natural light to pour in, creating a seamless blend of the inside and the outside world. As you sit down, you feel peaceful, as if the cottage is embracing you.

As you're relaxing, you hear a gentle knock at the door. You rise and open it, finding yourself face-to-face with your compassionate self. This figure is a version of you bathed in gentle light, a manifestation of unconditional love and understanding. This is the part of you that offers empathy, patience, and an unwavering acceptance of your entire being. It's a reminder that within you exists a source of endless compassion, ready to support you through any challenges you face.

You invite this compassionate presence into your cottage, and together, you sit in a space filled with warmth and light. Engage in a dialogue with your compassionate self. Tell them what you're thinking and feeling right now. Just let yourself say whatever comes to mind. This is your opportunity to express anything that weighs heavily on your heart, knowing it will be received with kindness and empathy. Speak openly, allowing the words to flow freely, knowing that you are in a place of absolute safety. Take your time to say all that is on your mind right now.

Now listen to the responses from your compassionate self, which offers a profound understanding. Your compassionate self says, "You are safe here. It's okay to feel what you are feeling. Your pain is valid, but it does not define you. You have the strength to heal and move forward. Remember, you are not alone. There are people who care about you and support you. Do not be critical of yourself. You did the best you could. Be gentle as you navigate this healing journey."

These words fill you with a warm, reassuring glow. You feel the love and acceptance from your compassionate self, wrapping around you like a comforting blanket. You are reminded that no matter what happens, you are loved. Take a moment to sit with these feelings, allowing them to wash over you and sink deeply into your being.

Your compassionate self tells you that you will overcome any difficulties and that you will heal. Now, your compassionate self gives you a gift, which is a word or phrase that resonates deeply within you. It's a mantra you can use in your healing journey that will help you when you need it most. Perhaps it is a single word like "strength" or "peace," or maybe a short phrase like "I am enough" or "I am loved." Take a moment to hear this mantra. Listen to them and then repeat it to yourself. Embrace this gift with gratitude, knowing it will help on your journey.

Your compassionate self embraces you and then leaves the cottage. Take a moment to absorb all that has occurred and to enjoy the serenity of this place. It is a refuge you can always return to whenever you need it. Know that this sanctuary, and the compassionate presence within it, is always available to you.

Take a deep breath as you leave the cottage, turning the key in the door. Recall the mantra and repeat it to yourself as you head down the path into the forest. The journey back through the forest feels different now, filled with a renewed sense of peace and strength.

Now, come back to your present environment, carrying these feelings into the day or evening.

Meditation Journey Thirty-Three: Healing Waters

Find a quiet and comfortable place to sit, somewhere you feel safe and at peace. Begin by focusing on your breathing. Take a deep breath in through your nose, feeling your lungs expand, and then slowly exhale. Let go of any tension or discomfort in your body.

Allow your shoulders to drop, your jaw to unclench, and your body to loosen. Feel the tension melting away, guiding you into a deeper state of relaxation with every deep breath you take.

Now, imagine that you have arrived at a special place—a serene water pool with a striking shade of bright blue. This isn't an ordinary pool; it's a place of healing and transformation. The pool is within a unique spa designed specifically to help those who have experienced trauma.

As you approach the water, you notice that the pool's surface is perfectly still. The water has a unique, almost magical quality, shimmering in the light. You slowly step into the pool, feeling the warm water envelop your feet. The temperature is perfect—neither too hot nor too cold. It immediately puts you at ease. As you immerse yourself completely in the water, you feel it supporting you as you float. The sensation is soothing and gentle, helping you to relax even more.

The healing waters flow gently around you, giving you a sense of safety and security. This is a space where you can acknowledge the trauma you've experienced without fear or judgment. As you think of this trauma, allow yourself to sit with the emotions that may arise—whether they are pain, fear, sadness, or anger. These feelings are a natural response to what you've been through, and it's important to recognize them. Know that in this space, your emotions are valid, and it's okay to feel them fully.

As feelings of fear and pain surface, you notice the surrounding water darken slightly. The pool is absorbing these emotions from you. In this moment, you remind yourself, "These fears are part of me, but they do not control me. It's understandable to feel this fear, but I can release its hold on me." As you acknowledge these thoughts, the water changes, transitioning to a lighter shade of blue. You feel a sense of relief washing over you as the water lightens, showing that some of the fear has been released.

Next, feelings of sadness may arise, and once again, the water darkens. The healing water is doing its work, drawing out these feelings and helping you process them. You might think to yourself, "I allow myself to feel this sadness, but I do not need to hold on to it. It's okay to feel sad, but I can also let it go." As the water absorbs the sadness, it gradually returns to a lighter, more vibrant blue. With each exhale, you feel the sadness easing.

As you continue to relax, you may notice feelings of self-blame or guilt. The surrounding water darkens slightly as these feelings arise in you. Gently remind yourself, "I am not to blame for what happened. I do not need to feel guilty." The healing waters respond, pulling these emotions away from you and replacing them with compassion and understanding. The water transitions from a dark navy to a brighter shade of blue, symbolizing the release of guilt and self-blame.

Shame may also make an appearance, whispering thoughts of unworthiness. As these feelings arise, the water momentarily darkens, and you counter them by saying, "These thoughts are not true. I deserve love and kindness." The water once again lightens as it absorbs these debilitating thoughts, leaving you with a sense of acceptance and self-worth.

Feelings of anger may also occur. The water darkens, mirroring the intensity of your emotions. Acknowledge this anger by thinking, "My anger is justified, but it does not help me heal. It's understandable for me to be angry, but I'm ready to let it go." As you release this anger, the water gradually lightens, taking the intensity of the emotion with it. You feel a deep breath of relief as the anger dissipates, leaving you feeling lighter and calmer.

Now, the water around you transitions to a soothing light blue color. It feels as though the water is embracing you, its gentle currents caressing your skin and soothing your soul. The warmth of the water penetrates deeply, relaxing your muscles and easing any remaining tension. You feel weightless, supported by the healing waters, and free from the burdens you've been carrying. Every movement you make sends gentle ripples through the pool, a reminder of the support and care surrounding you.

The water slowly changes to a pure white color, symbolizing purity and renewal. This transformation signifies a powerful shift toward self-compassion. The water feels magical, offering comfort and reassurance without words. It bubbles gently, as if speaking to you through its warmth and touch, communicating a deep sense of love and kindness. You think to yourself, "I am cared for and loved; I can heal." These waters, full of compassion, are working to heal the wounds of trauma, both seen and unseen.

You take this time to reflect on your inner strength and resilience. Acknowledge the courage it took to endure and survive the trauma you've faced. You are a survivor, and your strength is a testament to your spirit. You envision your future, a future where you are free from the shadows of trauma. See yourself living the life you desire, full of joy and fulfillment. Picture yourself surrounded by love and happiness, engaging in activities that bring you peace and contentment. The water around you returns to its original bright blue, signaling that the healing process has worked its magic.

Feeling rejuvenated and at peace, you slowly step out of the pool and stand outside of it. The water on your skin evaporates instantly, leaving you dry and comfortable. You feel lighter, both physically and emotionally, reassured that healing is a journey, and you are progressing one step at a time.

Now it's time to leave the healing pool. Come back to your present environment, taking these feelings into your day or evening.

Chapter 11: Embracing the Experience of Aging

Society often pressures us to resist aging, glorifies youthfulness, and suggests that we should view aging with trepidation. However, aging is the inevitable journey we all embark upon. It's a path marked by challenges and profound moments of growth, both daunting and deeply rewarding. In this chapter, I hope to help you on this journey, acknowledging that the passage of time may bring its trials, but it also offers wisdom, beauty, and opportunities for self-discovery.

When we face physical changes, losing loved ones, or shifting roles and responsibilities, we can embrace the journey with grace. Aging is not just a testament to a life lived, but an opportunity to savor the richness of existence. Wrinkles and gray hairs are not merely signs of aging; they result from life's laughter, tears, and adventures. And we should celebrate and appreciate making it to a certain age, particularly when not everyone is given that opportunity.

It's important to have self-compassion as you navigate the experience of aging. Embracing the changes that come with the passing years can lead to profound self-acceptance and fulfillment. We should celebrate growing older, recognizing that our later years provide a unique perspective to appreciate life's offerings. These years also present opportunities to share our wisdom, support others, and play a special role in the lives of our family and friends.

The meditation journeys in this chapter will help you navigate the journey of aging with compassion. After all, no matter where we are in our life's journey, we are all navigating the inevitable process of aging.

Meditation Journey Thirty-Four: The River of Life

Find a quiet place where you can relax and take a few deep breaths. Inhale and exhale slowly. Allow each breath to ease your body and calm your mind, releasing any tension you may be holding. Remind yourself that in this moment, there is nowhere else you need to be and nothing else you need to do. This is the time for you to reconnect with yourself.

As you continue to breathe deeply, envision yourself beside a gently flowing river, a symbol of your life's journey. The river winds through various landscapes, sometimes meandering lazily, reflecting more peaceful times in your life. At other times, the water rushes with urgency and power, representing the challenges and intense experiences you've faced. Each change in the river's pace reflects the varied experiences of your life, from the slow, quiet moments to the intense, fast-paced periods.

Lush grassy banks border the river and rolling hills surround it, symbolizing the richness and diversity of your life. The greenery signifies growth and renewal, while the hills represent the difficulties you have encountered along the way. As you sit upon the bank, enjoy the natural sounds—the gentle river flowing across rocks and the occasional chirping of birds. The warmth of the sun on your face and the freshness of the air make you feel connected to the natural world around you.

You take a moment to watch how the river interacts with its surroundings. The river polishes stones, smoothening their rough edges over time, just as your experiences have shaped and refined you. The banks are shaped by the flow, much like your life has been molded by both the gentle and challenging moments. You reflect on the natural barriers the river encounters—fallen trees, large rocks, or narrow passages—and how it navigates around them. Similarly, your life has faced obstacles, yet you have always found a way through, demonstrating resilience and adaptability.

As you admire the deep-blue river, the sun's gentle rays warm your body, prompting you to think about your own physical journey. You consider the ways your body has changed over the years, the wear it shows, and the signs of age it carries. Your hands bear lines etched from a lifetime of living, working, and loving. These lines are not just signs of aging; they are markers of your unique journey, a testament to the many experiences you've had. Your skin, softer and perhaps more fragile than before, carries wrinkles and spots, each one a silent witness to the time you've embraced.

You think about the changes in your strength and stamina, the different ways your body moves and rests now compared to earlier years. These changes are not just physical; they represent a deeper narrative of your life. Every ache and scar, every mark and line, tells a story of survival and resilience. As you reflect on this, you feel a deep sense of self-compassion and appreciation for your body and all it has done for you. It has been your faithful companion, enduring the ups and downs of life, adapting to changes, and continuing to serve you in countless ways.

You take a deep breath, inhaling acceptance and exhaling any harsh judgments you've held against your body. With each breath, you invite waves of compassion to flow through you, soothing and healing any discomforts. You relax into this moment, appreciating your body's continued efforts to provide you with life, despite the challenges it may face. You acknowledge the strength it takes to endure, and you honor this resilience with gratitude and respect.

As you continue to breathe deeply, a profound feeling of gratitude washes over you. See this feeling as a gentle, golden light radiating from your heart, spreading warmth and love to every part of your body. This light soothes aches, calms inflammation, and rejuvenates tired limbs. With each breath, you deepen your appreciation for your body. This moment of gratitude is a powerful acknowledgment of your body's enduring vitality, even as it adapts to the passage of time.

You watch the river and notice several twigs and leaves floating downstream. Some get caught in the eddies while others continue their journey unimpeded. This reminds you of the cognitive changes you've noticed over the years. Perhaps your memory isn't as sharp as it once was, or you find it takes longer to recall names, faces, or details. These changes are like the river's undercurrents—subtle yet influential, shaping the flow without always being visible on the surface.

As you breathe in deeply, you draw in compassion for your mind. Just like your body, your brain has undergone its own journey of growth and adaptation. With each inhale, you fill your mind with kindness, accepting these changes as natural parts of life's continuous flow. You consciously release any frustration or sadness these cognitive changes may have brought. Let go of self-criticism and internal pressure, imagining each breath as a wave of warmth and understanding washing over you, soothing anxiety and quieting harsh judgments.

As you sit by the river, you reflect on the emotional losses and farewells you've faced—loved ones who have passed, dreams that have shifted or faded, parts of your former self you have left behind. These experiences are like deep pools along the river's course, places where the water gathers strength before continuing its journey. You acknowledge that loss is an inevitable aspect of life, yet you also recognize that life, like the river, flows onward. Each loss has shaped you, adding depth and complexity to your journey.

Sitting by this river, you think of all that you have endured—the physical, cognitive, and emotional challenges. You recognize the persistence and resilience you've demonstrated, much like the river that flows ceaselessly despite obstacles.

The river does not flow in isolation; it is nourished by streams and rain, embraced by the banks that guide its course. In your own life, think of the support you've received from friends, family, and acquaintances. This network of people has been integral to your journey, reminding you that you are not alone. Take a moment to feel gratitude for all these supportive people.

Allow yourself a few more moments by the river, letting the sounds of the water, the warmth of the sun, and the tranquility of the setting envelop you. This river, with all its bends and breaks, flows on beautifully—just as you do.

Now it's time to leave. Come back to your present environment, carrying the calm and reflection of this moment with you.

Meditation Journey Thirty-Five: The Book of Life

Find a comfortable and quiet space to sit where you can completely unwind. Take a few moments to settle into a relaxed position, letting your body find a natural and comfortable posture. Start by taking a few deep breaths. Inhale deeply through your nose, feeling the air fill your lungs, expanding your chest and abdomen. Hold your breath for a moment, then exhale slowly. Repeat this process a few times, letting each breath anchor you and help you sink deeper into a state of relaxation.

Now, imagine entering an ancient, majestic library. As you step inside, you're greeted by the warm, earthy scent of aged paper and polished wood. The library is grand and timeless, a place that seems to hold the wisdom of ages. You're surrounded by towering bookshelves made of dark, polished wood that reach up to the arched ceilings high above. This canopy of rich, dark wood creates an atmosphere of reverence. The walls are lined with books of all sizes and colors, their spines bearing titles that span countless subjects and eras.

Tall, arched windows are set high above the enormous bookshelves, allowing streams of sunlight to pour into the room. The light filters through the windows, casting a white glow on the stone floor that creates a hazy luminescence. This ethereal light bathes the library in a serene, almost magical atmosphere.

As you walk down the central aisle, your footsteps echo softly on the stone floor. On either side of you are rows of antique wooden tables, each one inviting you to sit and explore the treasures this library holds. These tables are adorned with vintage brass lamps, their bases ornately decorated. Scattered across the tables are open books, their pages waiting to share their secrets with anyone who wishes to delve into them.

You choose a table and take a seat, feeling the smooth wood beneath your hands. As you sit down, you feel the weight of the world slip from your shoulders. Here, in this ancient library, you are free from the demands and distractions of daily life. The silence is profound, offering a rare opportunity for introspection. You take a deep breath, inhaling the calming scent of the old books and the wood, and as you exhale, you feel yourself becoming even more relaxed. This is a place where great minds have pondered, learned, and created great works.

As you settle in, you find yourself drawn to a particular book lying open on the table in front of you. The book is bound in weathered burgundy leather, its cover soft and worn from years of handling. Embossed in gold on the cover are the words: *The Book of Your Life*. The title intrigues you, and you feel a sense of curiosity. As you gently turn the pages, a soft, golden light emanates from the book.

This book contains the story of your life, beginning with your birth and early years. As you look at these pages, you see vivid images from that time—your first steps, your first words, the people who loved and cared for you. The book captures the essence of these memories, bringing them to life before your eyes. Each image, each memory, is precious. You see the major events that marked your early years and the simple, everyday moments that also hold a special place in your heart. You feel a deep sense of gratitude for these experiences and the love that surrounded you.

As you turn the pages, the book chronicles your childhood and adolescence. You see the places you lived, the schools you attended, and the teachers who influenced you. The pages are filled with memories of friendships and adventures, moments of joy and discovery. You recall the games you played, the lessons you learned, and the challenges you faced. Your heart swells with gratitude for the friends who shared these formative years with you. The book also brings to mind the flutter of first crushes and early romances, those tender and sometimes awkward moments that were part of growing up. Each of these experiences, big and small, has contributed to your development, shaping the person you are today.

You see your adult years—those spent in school or training. See yourself studying, learning, striving to master skills that would later prove invaluable. You remember the mentors who guided you and the friends who shared those hopeful days, all of you looking toward the future with anticipation.

The book then delves into the chapters that chronicle your work life. Here, you see the aspirations you pursued, the goals you set, and the accomplishments you achieved. You remember the important supervisors, colleagues, and mentors who guided and supported you along the way. These individuals played a significant role in your professional journey, helping you to grow and succeed. Each page reveals the deepening of your professional identity, the challenges you faced, and the triumphs you celebrated. You feel a sense of pride and fulfillment as you look back on these achievements, recognizing the hard work and dedication that brought you to where you are today.

The book also captures the important relationships in your adult life. You see the people who have been your companions, your confidants, and your loves. You remember the warmth of love and the lessons learned from heartaches. The enduring relationships have been gifts, teaching you about the depth of your own capacity to love and the qualities you value in others. For all these connections, both brief and lasting, you feel deeply grateful.

You also acknowledge the people who have touched your life in smaller, but still meaningful ways—the acquaintances who offered kindness, the strangers who provided help in moments of need. These interactions, though fleeting, have left an indelible mark on you.

As you continue to turn the pages, you reach the current chapter of your life. You realize that this present moment is a precious gift. It is an opportunity to fully appreciate the richness of life, to embrace the present with gratitude and openness. The book's pages contain no images or writing. They are not yet filled; there is still so much more to experience, to learn, and to love. You feel a sense of excitement for the future, knowing that each new day is a chance to add to the story of your life.

With a deep sense of peace and gratitude, you close The Book of Your Life. The ancient library has offered you a moment of reflection and introspection, a chance to honor the journey you've traveled and to look forward to the path ahead.

Now it's time to leave the library. Carry the feelings of peace, gratitude, and reflection with you into your day or evening.

Meditation Journey Thirty-Six: Celebration of Your Life

Take a moment to sit in a comfortable position and take a deep breath. Inhale slowly and then exhale even more slowly. Take several deep breaths, allowing yourself to relax onto the surface you're sitting on. When you're ready, we'll transition to a place where a group has gathered to celebrate you.

Imagine you're at the end of your life. Your closest friends and family members have come together to celebrate your life, but this is not a sad occasion. They're here to share wonderful memories and describe the impact you've had on their lives. They have so much to say, and they want you to hear it while you're still alive.

You walk down a long hallway and enter a large reception room adorned with flowers and brightly colored balloons. People from all different parts of your life fill the room. Banners with your name in vibrant colors hang prominently, setting a festive tone. The room hums with joyful energy as everyone is eager to make this a celebration of you rather than a somber event. These are your relatives and friends, people you love, and even those who have passed on—whose words will be read by the living.

As you enter the room, everyone applauds. "We want you to hear what we think and feel while you're still alive," one of your family members says. People stand in small groups, chatting before the meal, and you move through the crowd, greeting everyone. As you make your way around the room, people embrace you and say how glad they are to be here. Individuals of all ages are present, from the very young to older adults. There are people from every stage of your life—childhood, young adulthood, middle age, and your most recent years. See those you've worked with, socialized with, and lived near. All the people whose lives you've touched are here, including some surprises—faces you haven't seen in a long time.

You take a seat of honor, and everyone sits down. Servers bring in dishes you love, and the delicious scents fill the air as they place the food in front of everyone at the long tables. You're seated with beloved family members and your closest friends, who smile at you as they eat. Plate after plate of your favorite entrees and side dishes are served, and everyone enjoys these dishes. Then desserts are brought to the table—all your favorites. You decide to splurge and try several desserts, savoring the rich flavors.

Now comes the main event. Everyone turns toward the front of the room where one of your loved ones addresses the crowd, explaining that this is a celebration of your life. Many people want to share their heartfelt words and to express their gratitude to you.

As the first person steps up, you feel a wave of warmth and anticipation. It's your childhood friend, someone who holds a special place in your heart. They begin by sharing stories of your early years together, reminiscing about the adventures and innocent mischief you both got into. They speak of your kindness and the strong bond you shared, describing various memories that paint a vivid picture of those formative times. Their words highlight the traits that hinted at the wonderful person you would grow to become.

Then, a series of family members take turns speaking before the crowd, each sharing their unique perspectives and memories. One relative begins by reflecting on the holidays, recalling the warmth and joy you brought to family gatherings. They describe the festive decorations, the delicious meals, and the way you made everyone feel at home.

Your children, siblings, and other relatives recount times when you were a pillar of strength during challenging moments. They mention how your calm demeanor and encouraging words provided comfort and guidance, helping the family navigate through difficult situations. They emphasize your unwavering love and the way you always seemed to know the right thing to say or do to lift their spirits.

As each family member speaks, they capture the essence of your role within the family—not just as a relative, but as a friend, mentor, and confidant. The stories they share illustrate the depth of the bonds you nurtured and the profound impact you had on each of their lives. Through their eyes, the crowd gains a deeper understanding of the love, respect, and admiration you inspired in those who knew you best.

Your parents are present in spirit, and their words are read to the crowd. They describe what it was like to raise you and how much they loved you. Other dear people who have passed on also have their words read, recalling the many memories you created together and the impact you had on them. A tear comes to your eye as you listen to these heartfelt messages, but you find comfort knowing that love transcends all barriers.

Following them, a dear friend takes the stage. They share tales of the support and encouragement you provided during uncertain times and how your friendship was a source of strength and joy. The stories they tell remind everyone of the deep connections and unwavering loyalty you offered to those you loved.

Next, a colleague steps forward. They recount the challenges and triumphs you faced together in the workplace. They speak of your dedication, your ability to lead, and the way you made everyone feel valued and appreciated. A former coworker shares how you made the workplace more enjoyable and productive. They talk about the ways you affected them and the organization.

As the event continues, people from various stages of your life come forward to share their memories. Friends from different social circles, neighbors, and an old classmate talk about how you helped them. A child, now grown, remembers how you always took the time to listen, treating them with the same respect and care as you did your own family.

Finally, someone you once helped in a time of need takes the stage. They tell a story of compassion and generosity, of how you supported them when they needed it most. Their heartfelt words underscore the profound difference you made in their life, a testament to your kindness and empathy.

The celebration culminates with a collective expression of gratitude. Applause fills the room, and you feel a deep sense of fulfillment and peace. This gathering reflects your legacy, one that will continue to inspire and resonate for generations to come.

Conclusion: Embracing Self-Kindness Daily

Now that you have reached the final chapter, it's essential to understand that self-compassion is not a onetime endeavor; it's a lifelong practice. We should not reserve self-compassion only for moments of crisis or difficulty. It's a gift you can offer yourself every day, regardless of circumstances. Here's how to make it a natural part of your daily life.

- **Morning Reflection**: Start your day with a moment of self-reflection. Express gratitude for yourself and set an intention to be compassionate to yourself and others for the day ahead.
- **Mindful Awareness**: Throughout the day, cultivate mindfulness. Be aware of your thoughts and self-talk. Be mindful of the language you use when speaking to yourself. Replace harsh self-criticism with gentle and understanding words.
- **Self-Care Rituals**: Make self-care practices a regular part of your day. These can be activities like enjoying a warm bath, taking a walk in nature, or spending quiet time in contemplation.

Tips for Maintaining Self-Compassion

Maintaining self-compassion is essential for making self-kindness a lasting and transformative part of your life. Below are some tips to help you.

- **Consistency is Key**: Like any skill, self-compassion benefits from consistency. Establish a regular schedule for your self-compassion practices.
- **Self-Compassion Communities**: Consider joining self-compassion communities or online groups. Connecting with like-minded individuals who are also on their self-compassion journey can provide inspiration, insights, and a sense of belonging.
- **Patience**: Understand that self-compassion, like any skill, takes time to develop fully. Be patient with yourself as you navigate the difficulties of your journey. Remember that it's okay to have moments of self-doubt or self-criticism; what matters is how you respond with self-compassion.
- **Self-Reflect**: Periodically take time to reflect on your self-compassion journey. Journal about your experiences, insights, and challenges. Self-reflection can deepen your understanding of yourself and your relationship with self-kindness.
- **Gratitude**: Cultivate gratitude for the progress you've made on your self-compassion journey. Celebrate even the smallest steps. Acknowledge your growth and let gratitude fuel your motivation to continue.

The goal is to make self-compassion a lifestyle rather than a mere practice. Infuse self-kindness into every aspect of your life, from your self-talk to your interactions with others. Let self-compassion become a natural response to life's challenges and joys.

In this final chapter, I've included some additional meditation journeys to help you continue your journey.

Meditation Journey Thirty-Seven: Opening the Door to a New Life

Find a quiet space and sit comfortably. Take a few deep breaths, letting your shoulders drop as you relax into the support beneath you. Inhale slowly, allowing each breath to bring you into a state of tranquility. Continue taking several additional deep breaths, feeling the tension ease out of your body.

Imagine you're standing at the entrance of a long, softly lit hallway. This hallway represents your life's journey. The walls display major memories from your past, both joyful and challenging. Walking down this hallway, you see these important images of your life. Perhaps you see your wedding, the first time you met someone significant, scenes from family gatherings, or

171

interactions with friends. Maybe there are some painful moments, alongside joyful glimpses. Observe these moments without judgment; they are integral parts of your unique story.

With each step, you move closer to the ornate wooden door at the end of the hall, an entrance to a life filled with self-compassion. As you walk toward it, release the weight of self-criticism and past regrets. You declare, "I release my inner critic." With a few more steps, you say, "I forgive my past errors. I look forward to the future."

You feel lighter with each step, knowing that you are creating a space for self-compassion. Stand before this dark wooden door intricately carved with decorative motifs that catch the light. Its rich wooden frame boasts ornate designs and golden accents, reflecting a sense of grandeur. As you take in the sight of this exquisite door, you feel a sensation of anticipation and curiosity. What lies beyond this door is a realm of self-compassion and acceptance.

You place your hand on the ornate metal doorknob in the center of the door and turn it gently. The door opens easily, and you step into a world bathed in warm, compassionate light. Around you, the green landscape is vibrant and alive. Delicate flowers reach for the sky with intense colors, symbolizing growth and reaching one's full potential. Trees arch overhead, their branches a canopy of green, representing strength and stability. The ground beneath your feet is soft and yielding, carpeted with lush grass that cushions every step, reminding you that the path to self-compassion is supported by the earth itself. In this place, every breath creates feelings of tranquility. The air carries the sweet fragrance of jasmine and lavender, calming your mind.

There is a powerful energy of self-kindness that is palpable—you can feel it surrounding you. This environment soothes any lingering shadows of doubt and insecurity. As you breathe deeply, the energy of compassion fills you, transforming your view of yourself and your relationship with the world. Ahead of you, three paths lie in front of you. To the left is a path leading into a small forest where brightly colored birds flit about. In the center of the garden, a winding cobblestone path leads to a set of sunken gardens. These gardens contain roses of every imaginable hue—soft pinks, vibrant reds and violets, sunny yellows, and pure whites. To the right is a path leading to a beautiful brick mansion. Each of these places is yours to explore. Choose the path that speaks to you.

As you walk along, you see signs on the side of the path with messages:

"Embrace your imperfections with kindness and understanding."

"Offer yourself the gift of self-compassion."

"You are enough, just as you are."

These signs reinforce your desire to be more compassionate toward yourself. As you explore this world, you trip over something unseen and stumble to the ground. You are not hurt, but you chastise yourself. Then, you stop. You silence your inner critic and say, "Everyone stumbles. I'm okay. Everyone makes mistakes. That is just part of life." You pick yourself up and continue walking along the path.

As you walk towards the mansion, the garden, or the forest, you think about your life. Each step brings a renewed commitment to being more compassionate to yourself. You imagine responding to life's challenges not with frustration or impatience, but with a calm understanding that every obstacle is an opportunity to learn and grow. You envision moments where, instead of succumbing to deriding yourself, you acknowledge everyone has challenges and everyone makes mistakes.

See yourself taking time for self-care—whether it's a quiet walk, a rest, or doing an activity that brings you joy. Imagine replacing harsh judgments with gentle words of encouragement, offering yourself the same kindness you would extend to a dear friend. When feelings of frustration or inadequacy arise, hear a calm voice within you saying, "Some things are hard, and I will tackle this. It may take time, but I'll do it."

You explore the garden, forest, and mansion. This is your world, filled with wonderful scenery and a warm, accepting atmosphere. It is a place you can always return to whenever you need it. Take as long as you need to experience this wonderful place. The forest, with its vibrant birds and inviting paths, symbolizes exploration and growth. Sunken gardens, with their fragrant flowers, represent the beauty and variety of life. The brick mansion stands as a testament to the strength and stability you carry within.

As you wander through this realm, feel the warm, compassionate light infusing every part of you. When you're ready to return, simply turn around and walk back through the door you entered. The hallway is still there, adorned with the memories of your life, but now you see them with fresh eyes. Each memory is a lesson, each experience is a step on your journey. You walk confidently, knowing that you have the wisdom to navigate whatever lies ahead.

Now it's time to come back to your present environment. As you come back, carry the vision of this new life with you.

Meditation Journey Thirty-Eight: Cultivating a Garden of Self-Compassion

Begin by finding a tranquil, comfortable space where you can relax and take time for yourself. Take several deep breaths. Inhale slowly, then exhale slowly. Take several of these soothing breaths to center your mind and body.

Imagine you are in a garden with many beds, carrying a basket filled with seeds. These seeds are not ordinary; they are the seeds of understanding, forgiveness, patience, love, and kindness—elements of self-compassion. The garden is beautifully arranged with a series of open beds, each bordered by natural stone and filled with rich, dark earth ready to nurture new growth. Winding paths lead you from one area of the garden to another, each section dedicated to a different virtue, creating a place of growth and healing.

You first come to a bed designated for understanding. Here, you plant the seeds in neat rows. As you place each seed in the earth and cover it gently with soil, you say, "May I be understanding toward myself and others. We are all navigating our paths as best as we can." Feel the energy of understanding grow with each seed planted. The sun shines down, and as you repeat these words, small lavender plants rise from the soil, their soft purple flowers swaying gently in the breeze, releasing a soothing scent that fills the air.

Next, you move to the forgiveness section of the garden. This area feels tranquil, shaded lightly by the overhanging branches of an enormous tree nearby. You sow these seeds of forgiveness with a sense of relief, each one falling to the ground, symbolizing a past hurt you are releasing. As you cover these seeds, you whisper, "May I forgive myself and others, letting go of burdens and welcoming peace." As you feel forgiveness growing within yourself, green ferns sprout up, displaying their many small leaves and beautiful arching fronds, symbolizing the delicate yet resilient nature of letting go and moving forward.

The bed of patience is next, by a gently trickling stream. The sound of the water is calming and rhythmic. As you plant these seeds, you say, "May I have patience with myself and others, understanding that all things unfold in their own time." You breathe deeply, glance at the slowly moving stream, and feel a sense of patience within you. The seeds take root, grow, and give rise to bamboo, their tall, slender stalks reaching upward, symbolizing strength and flexibility.

In the heart of the garden is the bed for love. Here, the soil seems warmer, the air filled with an earthy fragrance. You plant these seeds deeply, with intention and care, saying, "May I love myself unconditionally, knowing that true compassion starts within." As you repeat this phrase, the area blossoms with roses of many vibrant colors, attracting bees and butterflies, a center of life and energy. The roses' petals are soft, their fragrance rich and inviting, embodying the essence of love and compassion.

Finally, you arrive at the section for kindness. The sunlight bathes this part of the garden, making it open and inviting. The bright light makes everything seem more vivid. As you plant these seeds, you say, "May I be kind to myself and to others, spreading warmth and joy wherever I go." As you feel kindness growing within, you see sunflowers emerging from the earth, their leaves reaching out like open hands, ready to brighten anyone's day with their cheerful faces. The sunflowers turn toward the sun, symbolizing positivity and warmth.

As you stroll through your garden, taking in the scents of the flourishing plants, you can sense these virtues blossoming within you. You wander along the winding path to the understanding section and watch the lavender growing out of the soil, filling the air with its distinctive scent as you repeat, "May I be understanding toward the many parts of my life." The lavender fragrance is calming, and its presence reminds you to be gentle with yourself and others.

Next, you visit the forgiveness garden bed where vibrant green ferns are growing. You say, "I forgive myself and others. Life is too short to hold on to negative feelings." The ferns' delicate leaves flutter lightly in the breeze, symbolizing the release of old grudges.

Now you go over to the patience bed where you see bamboo slowly rising and swaying with the wind. You say, "May I have patience with my challenges." The bamboo's sturdy stalks and gentle movements remind you that patience can make you stronger and more flexible.

Next, you wander to the center of the garden and visit the love bed, where you see roses that seem to unfold as you say, "May I approach my life and myself with love." The roses' vibrant colors and soft petals symbolize the beauty and power of self-love and compassion.

Finally, you go over to the kindness bed, where you see sunflowers that rise up and lean toward the sun as you say, "May I always be kind." The sunflowers' bright faces and tall stems represent the wonder that kindness brings into your life and the lives of others.

If any of the garden beds of understanding, forgiveness, patience, love, or kindness need extra attention, visit them again and nurture the plants by saying something that helps you cultivate that virtue. As you internalize these thoughts, the plants in each section will flourish and grow. You might whisper more words of encouragement to the lavender, coax the ferns to spread wider, encourage the bamboo to grow taller, admire the roses more closely, or bask in the brightness of the sunflowers.

You walk back to look at the entire garden from a distance and say, "I nurture myself with kindness and patience. I embrace forgiveness, understanding, and love." The entire garden now seems to shimmer with life, each section a testament to the virtues you have planted and are now cultivating within yourself.

Now it's time to leave your garden of self-compassion. Come back to your present environment, carrying with you the thoughts and feelings you cultivated in this garden. You can return to this garden anytime you need to reconnect with these virtues and rejuvenate your spirit.

Dear Reader,

Thank you so much for reading or listening to these meditation journeys.

As you continue your journey of self-compassion, I wish you all the best. I hope you keep using these journeys to make kindness towards yourself a natural reflex. Self-compassion is a powerful force that can brighten your days and positively affect those around you.

I wish you a wonderful life filled with happiness and all the love you deserve.

Warmly,

Anne E. Beall, PhD

Anne E. Beall, PhD

Anne E. Beall is an award-winning author whose books have been featured in *People Magazine*, *Chicago Tribune*, *Toronto Sun*, *Hers Magazine*, *Ms. Career Girl*, and she's been interviewed by NBC, NPR, and WGN. Her book, *Cinderella Didn't Live Happily Ever After: The Hidden Messages in Fairy Tales* won a Gold award from Literary Titan. Her book, *Only Prince Charming Gets to Break the Rules* won a Silver award from Literary Titan. And her *Heartfelt Connections* book was named one of the top 100 Notable Indie books in 2016 by *Shelf Unbound*. She has published in several literary journals including *Minerva Rising Press*, *The Raven's Perch*, and *Grande Dame Literary Journal*. She received her PhD in social psychology from Yale University and is the founder of the firm, Beall Research. She is deeply passionate about promoting emotional well-being for all people.

Additional Resources and Readings

You may find the following resources and readings valuable. These books, websites, and courses offer further insights and guidance on the path to embracing self-compassion and kindness toward yourself.

Books

- *Self-Compassion: The Proven Power of Being Kind to Yourself* by Kristin Neff
- *The Gifts of Imperfection: Let Go of Who You Think You're Supposed to Be and Embrace Who You Are* by Brené Brown
- *Radical Acceptance: Embracing Your Life with the Heart of a Buddha* by Tara Brach
- *The Mindful Path to Self-Compassion: Freeing Yourself from Destructive Thoughts and Emotions* by Christopher K. Germer

Websites and Online Courses:

- Center for Mindful Self-Compassion (https://centerformsc.org/): Offers information on Mindful Self-Compassion (MSC) courses, workshops, and resources.
- Kristin Neff's Self-Compassion Website (https://self-compassion.org/): Dr. Kristin Neff's website provides research-based articles, exercises, and guided meditations on self-compassion.
- Brené Brown's Website (https://brenebrown.com/): Explore Brené Brown's work on vulnerability, courage, and wholehearted living.

Apps for Self-Compassion:
- Calm App (https://www.calm.com/): A meditation app with guided meditations that encourage self-compassion.
- Insight Timer app (https://insighttimer.com/): A meditation app with a wide range of guided meditations.
- Headspace app (https://www.headspace.com/): Offers mindfulness and self-compassion exercises to help you cultivate a compassionate mindset.

These resources are just a starting point, and there is a wealth of information and support available to you.

Sources

Bates GW, Elphinstone B, Whitehead R. (2021). Self-compassion and emotional regulation as predictors of social anxiety. *Psychology and Psychotherapy*. 94(3):426–442.

Bui THT, Nguyen TNT, Pham HD, Tran CT, Ha TH. (2021) The mediating role of self-compassion between proactive coping and perceived stress among students. *Science Progress*. 104(2).

Germer, C. K., & Neff, K. D. (2015). Cultivating self-compassion in trauma survivors. In V. M. Follette, J. Briere, D. Rozelle, J. W. Hopper, & D. I. Rome (Eds.), Mindfulness-oriented interventions for trauma: Integrating contemplative practices (pp. 43–58). The Guilford Press.

Mülazım, Öznur & Eldeleklioğlu, Jale. (2016). What is the role of self-compassion on subjective happiness and life satisfaction? *Journal of Human Sciences*. 13(3).

Neff, K. (2011). *Self-Compassion: Stop Beating Yourself Up and Leave Insecurity Behind*. HarperCollins Publishers.

Neff, K. D., & Beretvas, S. N. (2013). The role of self-compassion in romantic relationships. *Self and Identity*, 12(1), 78-98.

Neff, K. D., Hsieh, Y. P., & Dejitterat, K. (2005). Self-compassion, achievement goals, and coping with academic failure. *Self and Identity*, 4(3), 263-287.

Neff, K. D., Kirkpatrick, K. L., & Rude, S. S. (2007). Self-compassion and adaptive psychological functioning. *Journal of Research in Personality, 41*(1), 139-154.

Neff, K. D., Rude, S. S., & Kirkpatrick, K. L. (2007). An examination of self-compassion in relation to positive psychological functioning and personality traits. *Journal of Research in Personality*, 41(4), 908-916.

Oswald, A. J., Proto, E., and Sgroi, D. (2015) Happiness and productivity. *Journal of Labor Economics*, 33 (4). pp. 789-822.

Powers, T. A., Koestner, R., & Zuroff, D. C. (2007). Self-criticism, goal motivation, and goal progress. *Journal of Social and Clinical Psychology*, 26, 826-840.

Terry, M. L., Leary, M. R., Mehta, S., & Henderson, K. (2013). Self-compassionate reactions to health threats. *Personality and Social Psychology Bulletin*, 39(7), 911-926.